The
Good Cook's Book
of Tomatoes

Other Books by Michele Anna Jordan

More Than Meatballs

Vinaigrettes & Other Dressings

The World Is a Kitchen

Lotsa Pasta

VegOut! A Guide Book to Vegetarian Friendly Restaurants in Northern California

The BLT Cookbook

San Francisco Seafood

The New Cook's Tour of Sonoma

Pasta Classics

California Home Cooking

Polenta

Pasta with Sauces

Ravioli & Lasagne

The Good Cook's Journal

The Good Cook's Book of Mustard

The Good Cook's Book of Oil & Vinegar

The Good Cook's Book of Salt & Pepper

A Cook's Tour of Sonoma

The
Good Cook's Book
of Tomatoes

A NEW WORLD DISCOVERY AND ITS OLD WORLD IMPACT, WITH MORE THAN 150 RECIPES

MICHELE ANNA JORDAN

PHOTOGRAPHY BY LIZA GERSHMAN

FOREWORD BY FLO BRAKER

Skyhorse Publishing

Skyhorse Publishing books may be purchased in bulk at special discounts for
sales promotion, corporate gifts, fund-raising, or educational purposes. Special
editions can also be created to specifications. For details, contact the Special Sales
Department, Skyhorse Publishing, 307 West 36th Street, 11th Floor, New York,
NY 10018 or info@skyhorsepublishing.com.

Skyhorse® and Skyhorse Publishing® are registered trademarks of Skyhorse
Publishing, Inc.®, a Delaware corporation.

Visit our website at www.skyhorsepublishing.com.

10 9 8 7 6 5 4 3 2 1

Library of Congress Cataloging-in-Publication Data is available on file.

Cover design by Erin Seward-Hiatt
Cover photo credit Liza Gershman

Print ISBN: 978-1-63220-698-5
Ebook ISBN: 978-1-63450-017-3

Printed in China

"A world without tomatoes is like a string quartet without violins."

—Laurie Colwin, *Home Cooking: A Writer in the Kitchen*

for James Carroll and John Boland,

again and always

&

for the magnificent tomato farmers of Sonoma County,
who make my work a delicious joy

and

In memory of Professor Charles M. "Mr. Tomato" Rick
1915–2002

Contents

Part 2: The Annotated Tomato Pantry

Part 3: A Tomato Cookbook

Part 4: Appendices

Foreword

For as long as I can remember, I've had a passion for food. For me, cooking is one of life's great pleasures, and I believe that most of us want to feel relaxed and knowledgeable in the kitchen. Many of us want to cook with inspiration as well.

Just as an artist experiences a sense of well-being and an edge of excitement when sitting down with brushes, paints, and palette to create a new work, a cook likes to feel both confident and full of ideas when he or she opens the pantry, reaches for an apron, and begins cooking.

My idea of a great cookbook is one that, on opening it, I want to take to a quiet corner to read and savor, because I know immediately that it's going to give me lots of information, some new skills, and lasting inspiration.

Michele Jordan has written three such books: *The Good Cook's Book of Oil & Vinegar*, *The Good Cook's Book of Mustard*, and now *The Good Cook's Book of Tomatoes*. Her approach is to guide us to explore every facet of each essential ingredient in her grand collections of innovative recipes so that we can duplicate as well as experiment and to encourage us to use what we've learned. Today, all across America, consumers have an embarrassment of riches. So many new and unfamiliar vinegars, oils, mustards, and tomatoes are available that just shopping for a recipe can be a challenge. Michele gives us exactly the information we need to make intelligent choices so that we can work with these ingredients easily and skillfully and use them as a springboard for our own culinary creations.

Michele's three volumes are not just cookbooks to be quickly scanned in order to decide what to whip up for a meal. Instead, each book treats a particular ingredient so thoroughly that in the end you can almost taste

the recipes as you read them, and then go on to create countless variations of your own.

This fine trilogy of companion books weaves the vibrant tastes, textures, and aromas of everyday essential ingredients into well-organized information that appeals to the novice as well as to the experienced home cook. Each book begins with some historical, botanical, and commercial background on the ingredient, and even addresses pertinent health issues. A section called "The Annotated Pantry" includes Michele's personal comments and notes. Her recipes follow, and they are easy-to-prepare contemporary dishes that guarantee delicious results for every course of a meal.

Michele's glossary, "Tasting" section, and sample forms for conducting your own tastings are invaluable resources. Her easy-to-follow instructions on how to conduct comparative tastings educate your palate and give you faith in your own judgment. After all, that's what good cooking is all about—taste.

For me, though, perhaps the greatest pleasure in reading any one of *The Good Cook's* books is that Michele brings life to the ingredients that we tend to take for granted. After reading one of these books you will never again underestimate the power of a simple ingredient. Moreover, you'll want the entire series close to you in the kitchen as handy references to use again and again. Michele's passion jumps off each page and entices you to taste, experiment, and cook. Three cheers for *The Good Cook's* books: *Oil & Vinegar! Mustard! Tomatoes!*

Flo Braker
Palo Alto, 1995

Acknowledgments

A very special thanks goes to Nicole Frail of Skyhorse Publishing for making a crazy deadline schedule actually doable. Nicole, you are a joy to work with! Thanks, as well, to the entire Skyhorse team.

I could not have written this book, neither the first edition nor this one, were it not for the talented and dedicated farmers and gardeners of Sonoma County, who nurture their tomato plants from tender little seedlings to huge productive vines, giving us, in a good year, delicious heirloom and hybrid tomatoes from sometime in June all the way to mid-November. Special thanks goes to Lazaro Calderon of The Patch in Sonoma; Nancy Skall of Middleton Farms in Healdsburg; Cliff Silva of Ma & Pa's Garden in Sebastopol; Yael Bernier and her son Zureal of Bernier Farms in Geyserville; Susan and Lou Preston and their crew at Preston Farms and Winery in Healdsburg; Larry Tristano and his crew at Triple T Farms in Santa Rosa; and Adam Davidoff of New Family Farm in Sebastopol.

Thanks, as well, to Dominique Cortara of Dominique's Sweets, who made gorgeous tomato galettes for one of our photo sessions and has been a great friend through it all. Thanks for the bubbly, Dominique!

I am filled with gratitude for the talent and dedication of Paula Downing, who currently manages the Sebastopol Farmers Market and is responsible for transforming farmers markets in Sonoma County from good to extraordinary and extraordinarily successful. I've never met anyone who understands and loves farmers as much as Paula and I am deeply thankful for the wisdom she continues to share with all of us.

Dennis Dunn, who sells his brother's One World Sausage products at several farmers markets, has been understanding and supportive of this project, too; thanks, Dennis! And thanks to Franco Dunn for making some of the best sausages on the planet.

Andy Ross of the Andy Ross Agency is the nicest agent in the universe; he also is whip smart, funny, supportive, kind, and patient. Thanks bunches, Andy, for everything.

Liza Gershman's photographs bring life to my explorations of the love apple and beauty to my cooking. Thanks so much for working so hard, Liza, under such a grueling deadline and minuscule—by which I mean zero—budget.

In a timely burst of intuition, I asked a colleague, Rayne Wolfe, if she wanted to do some prop styling for our photo sessions. I knew only that she was a keen thrifter and handy with vintage materials and I think we were all surprised when she stepped into her new role as Prop Mistress without missing a beat. Thanks so much, Rayne.

I send big hugs and a big mahalo to my longtime friend and hula sister Nancy Lorenz, colleague Kelly Keagy, and grandson Lucas Rice Jordan, for helping with the photography, including preparation, organization, and the all-important cleanup.

Special thanks goes to Clark Wolf, for always sharing his wisdom and supporting my work, and to his radio co-host Marcy Smothers and their producer Scott Mitchell.

Merci beaucoup to my friends Steve Garner and John Ash of The Good Food Hour and Steve Jaxon of The Drive, and to Mike Young, Sean Knight, and Mary Moore-Campagna of KRCB-FM, where I have done my show, "Mouthful, the Wine Country's Most Delicious Hour," for nearly twenty years.

Finally, to my dear friends James Carroll and John Boland, my daughters Nicolle Jordan and Gina Jordan, my son-in-law Tom O'Brien, and my grandson Lucas, thank you, again, for everything.

Introduction
to the Second Edition

The world as we know it has been transformed since I wrote the first edition of *The Good Cook's Book of Tomatoes* in 1994. Then, the World Wide Web had been open to the public for just three years, Google didn't exist, and Steve Jobs had not yet returned to Apple. I relied on research librarians, snail mail, and my trusty landline telephone for research. I wrote the manuscript on a Mac LC using, if memory serves, OS7, printed it on an Apple laser printer for which I paid nearly $900, and mailed it to my editor in Boston, who mailed it back with editorial comments in red pencil. Back and forth it went, by snail mail, in various forms. Production took a full year after I delivered the completed manuscript.

The new edition has been researched, written, delivered, formatted, and edited entirely electronically and it feels as if I'm delivering the final pages moments before it flies off, electronically, to the printer.

This is how we live now.

There have been other transformations, too, and the most important one to this book is what has happened with tomatoes in America in these twenty-plus years. In 1993 and 1994, one had to search for good tomatoes. Certain areas, including where I live in Northern California, had innovative growers exploring heirloom varieties but many parts of the country were tomato wastelands. Now great tomatoes are everywhere, or almost, at farmers markets in every state, at farm stands, and in many markets around the country. Those cardboard-like out-of-season tomatoes still fill supermarket produce departments but there are much better alternatives now than there were then.

Still, the tomato is a stubborn creature that has defied nearly all attempts to rip it from its season. A few growers, including Kelley Parsons of Parsons Homegrown in Sonoma County, provide hothouse tomatoes during late winter and spring that are pretty good, especially when you must have them, as I did in February 2014, when I had to construct a sixty-four-foot-long BLT for a special event.

Mostly, I avoid tomatoes from early November until sometime in early summer, as I always have, believing that longing, that delayed gratification, heightens one's pleasure. I'd rather have perfectly succulent and flavorful tomatoes five months out of the year than mediocre tomatoes year-round. But when the season hits, it hits more colorfully, more gloriously, and more diversely than I recall. Gardeners and farmers have made tremendous strides in understanding what varieties of tomatoes grow best in which soils and what climates. You can now grow succulent tomatoes in foggy areas like San Francisco, thanks to the San Francisco Fog variety, or other similar tomatoes. There are delicious tomatoes for every purpose, including one that grows nearly hollow, perfect for stuffing.

This new edition also reflects my evolution as a cook. I've grown more confident, more focused, more steady on my feet, so to speak, when it comes to my particular style. I've also traveled extensively in the years since I wrote the book, which was my third. I've eaten, wandered farmers markets, and cooked both on hot plates and in spacious kitchens, in France, Italy, Sicily, Spain, Portugal, Poland, Germany, Scotland, England, Canada, Malaysia, and many parts of my own country—New York, Alaska, Mississippi, and Hawaii—where I had not previously lingered long enough to actually cook. Every trip, no matter how brief, has shaped who I am in the kitchen and at the table. It is a pleasure to share it all with you.

Introduction
to the First Edition

I

"What's the sequel to *Mustard* going to be?" a friend asked. "Ketchup?"

Very funny, I thought, but admitted that the answer was yes, sort of, even though the sweet, pungent tomato condiment we call ketchup was a walnut-based sauce in Europe centuries ago. Today, ketchup is synonymous with tomato.

The tomato has been one of my favorite foods since I can remember. The memory of each summer of my childhood is fragrant with red and golden vine-ripened tomatoes, many of them from my step-grandfather's garden, others from a farm stand on the edge of town. I ate them with abandon, took them for granted, considered them an essential fact of life, like rain in the winter or my birthday in July. It never occurred to me that a simple tomato, pure and sweet and silky, would ever be out of my grasp. That realization would come later, when I was a young mother and garden-grown tomatoes were harder and harder to come by. In the days of youthful abundance, they were simply a part of summer, like cherries, watermelon, and dark, juicy nectarines.

My most vivid memories of tomatoes are connected to bouts of childhood illnesses, when I would rest propped up on the couch with thick, deep pillows, pampered with juices and stories, but most of all, tempted with whatever I was willing to eat. My favorite sickbed meal consisted of tomatoes and beef, more suited perhaps to a Chicago steak house, but there you have it. A little steak was broiled very rare and cut into small pieces. Next to it would be similarly cut pieces of tomato, a little salt

sprinkled over the whole affair. I ate with limpid pleasure and drank the delicious juices that collected in the center of the plate.

Perhaps because tomatoes are among the most stubborn agricultural products, they are also one of the most esteemed. The tomato simply refuses to submit to our human efforts to bend it to our will, and thus a well-grown tomato bursting with its full flavor remains evocative of its season like few other fruits or vegetables. A taste of a tomato is like a taste of summer itself; its aroma and the scent of its leaves evoke warm days and golden sunlight. Even if we succeed in creating great-tasting tomatoes in, say, January, I question how right they will be when so far removed from their natural time. A tomato belongs to summer, and I say let's leave it there and preserve what we can in our freezers, dehydrators, and canning kettles to warm us through the winter months.

II

I called my friend Jerry the other evening. "What's happenin'?" I asked as I stirred onions and garlic simmering in olive oil. The aromas were wonderful, provocative, and ripe with promise.

"Making spaghetti," was the reply.

"The regular kind," I asked, "with onions and garlic and tomatoes?"

"That's the one," Jerry said, as I opened my can of crushed tomatoes and emptied it into the skillet.

A big pot of water was already boiling on the stove and a half pound of dry Italian spaghettini was sitting nearby. I'd sent my daughter Nicolle out to the garden to pick a little fresh oregano, and a chunk of Parmigiano-Reggiano rested on the cutting board.

Jerry and I are very different kinds of cooks. I've had dinner at his house that has included a salad with dozens of miniature marshmallows. He sometimes introduces me to friends, saying, "Hey, this is Michele. She had us to dinner and gave us vinegar ice cream for dessert." He laughs, and I keep quiet about marshmallows.

But over pots of spaghetti in our respective kitchens, our culinary paths intersect. I've never tasted Jerry's spaghetti, but I'll bet it's not all that different from mine. Strands of good semolina pasta cloaked in a mildly tart tomato sauce—what could be simpler, friendlier, more soothing and delicious? It is, for me anyway, the ultimate comfort food, better than cinnamon toast, more consoling than soup, infinitely yummier than anything made with chocolate.

I have eaten spaghetti at pivotal moments in my life and have sought solace in the simple preparation it requires. I have eaten spaghetti everywhere, at all times, and from as early as I can remember. I have eaten it at 4:00 a.m. in the hopes that it might prevent a hangover (it helps). I have eaten it in some of San Francisco's most expensive Italian restaurants, even though I knew I could have it at home the next day. I ate spaghetti in grammar school, from a wide-mouthed thermos when my mother finally caved in to my refusal to eat sandwiches. There have been times when I couldn't have it, like a long summer spent in India, when I ached with longing for the comfort it and nothing else provides.

A bite of spaghetti, or simply the sight of it, can trigger endless memories: spaghetti dinners on Halloween when my mother knew it was the one thing she could get me to eat; the time I first saw the Pacific Ocean on a school field trip and there was hot spaghetti waiting for me when I got home. On countless occasions in front of every refrigerator I've owned, I have eaten it with my fingers, cold, doused with Tabasco sauce and extra salt. I have stood in the refrigerator's ghostly light, gathered up a few gooey strands with my fingers, held my hand high above my head, and lowered the spaghetti into my mouth, letting its evocative power nourish my heart just as the sauce-covered noodles nourished my body.

III

"Hurry," I said to myself over and over in the spring of 1994 until the repetition sounded like an incantation. Hurry. I was impatient, eager, I thought, to be finished with this book and onto something else. As I finished a final edit of the manuscript, I realized that my impatience had not been with the book at all. It wasn't completion that I sought, though my deadline was very real. What I really wanted was for the season itself to hurry up, for the mild days of spring to give way to the heat of summer. I wanted a tomato. I longed for one with growing pensiveness, but as luck would have it, it was a cool spring and thus a slow harvest. The wait seemed interminable. I checked my plants daily, but the little globes remained hard and green. How difficult it was to detail a tomato's delightful qualities without having them readily at hand as I wrote.

Finally, as I tended to the last details, the first tomato in my garden turned a luxurious red; a second blushed a warm and rich yellow, and then a third and a fourth, and the season was under way. Suddenly, as happens every year just about the time I think I'll burst with longing, wonderful tomatoes were everywhere. I set aside the wintery sauces, soups, and stews I'd been making with last year's harvest—so welcome in January, so dull by June—and began my yearly indulgence in gooey tomato sandwiches slathered with mayonnaise; delicate sliced tomatoes drizzled with luscious olive oil, topped with sweet red onions, creamy mozzarella cheese, silvery sardines. I called a friend and invited him over for savory tomato pie, still fragrant and warm from the oven.

On the warmest days, I stayed cool with bowls of gazpacho.

There was always plenty of fresh salsa.

For just three or four months—a little more if we're lucky— tomatoes are in such glorious abundance. I eat them every day, trying to get my fill before the first frost. Of course, I never succeed, and as the last of the year's tomatoes turn mushy with fall's first frost, the longing begins all over again, even as their taste lingers on my tongue. And so this book, the third in *The Good Cook's* series, is both an invocation and an invitation. Understand the nature of the tomato as a seasonal creature. Celebrate it, but as the days grow cold and the true tomato disappears, shun the substitutes that appear in the marketplace. Look instead to your pantry shelves and preserved tomatoes, and let the fire of longing build until, finally, there it will be next summer, and the summer after, the true tomato, tasting all the better because we've had to wait so long.

PART I
All about Tomatoes

Can anyone deny the compelling pleasure of a summer tomato plucked right off the vine, still warm from the sun, eaten right there in the garden? Oblivious to spurts of seeds and dripping juices, we are at one with nature as we devour our succulent morsel. Has anything ever tasted better?

Every eager eater has his or her own variation of this tomato story, a memory of a pivotal sensual encounter. Many a crusade has begun this way, in gardens and farm stands, over backyard fences, in markets in the south of France. We recognize a true tomato with our first bite, and we seek a second with the fervor of a knight after the Holy Grail. The true tomato, that is what we crave, and once we have savored it we do not live well without it.

There is a broad, even enthusiastic, consensus about what constitutes an authentically good tomato. The ideal tomato is heavy in the hand and has a pleasing, pungent aroma when we nuzzle close to it. It is encased in a thin skin that comes off easily should we decide to peel it (see sidebar, page 44). Should we cut it instead, it yields willingly beneath a sharp blade, without pressure or sawing. Once it is sliced, its flesh shines while small seed pockets glisten with thick gel. It feels silky to the tongue and its taste is both sweet and tangy. Our tomato is entirely pleasing and satisfying, though we can devour it and several of its comrades and not feel uncomfortably full. Our tomato offers pure, simple, sensual pleasure and gastronomic satisfaction. For the majority of people in the United States, it has become astonishingly hard to come by. Consumers' single greatest culinary lament is over the difficulty of finding good tomatoes, tomatoes "like they used to taste," tomatoes of what is generally called backyard quality.

There is little disagreement as to how to achieve a tomato of perfection. Follow a few elementary rules, and it is easy to end up with a daunting abundance of great tomatoes, much to the neighbors' delight. Articles and essays that praise the tomato do so in remarkably similar ways, evoking the pleasures of devouring the silky pulp in simple ways that accent the tomato's natural goodness. The suggestions of how and where and when to grow the best tomatoes are virtually the same as well, with subtle variations of variety, location, and method of cultivation, with specialized techniques developed by scores of award-winning home gardeners. But everyone agrees on the basic concept: tomatoes should be grown for flavor; they must ripen on their vines; they should be eaten soon after picking; and they must not be refrigerated. It is an uncomplicated equation and backyard gardeners achieve success with ease and satisfaction.

Why, then, has a good tomato been so hard to come by in a store? The demands of commercial farming—of getting the perishable little thing to the store, selling it at a price consumers will pay, and turning a profit— have diminished the pleasure the tomato once offered. For decades now, scientists and farmers have been relentlessly experimenting with tomatoes, seeking ways to deliver backyard flavor to the marketplace. Success has been limited, in spite of the ultimately simple solution: let the tomatoes ripen on the vine.

No one praises standard commercial tomatoes—thick-skinned, cottony lumps that are picked green and never really ripen but simply turn red with the application of ethylene gas. The abuse is increased, not that it makes much difference, during refrigerated transportation and cold storage in both warehouses and markets, which halts the ripening process, renders the flesh mealy, and lowers the vitamin content. The result is appalling, an insult to both the fruit itself and the person eating it. Although farmers

markets are increasingly available in all parts of the country, offering beautiful, flavorful tomatoes in season, the majority of Americans still rely on major markets for most of their shopping. Nearly every supermarket in the country features mounds of these pale, mushy tomatoes whose taste bears not even a shadowy resemblance to what we seek. Why, then, do they continue to sell in such numbers? Are those of us with taste buds that recall the tomato's true pleasure really in such small numbers? Is it impatience, our distance from the seasons, our refusal to accept the fresh tomato as a seasonal creature that make us demand it in January just as we crave it in July? Is it economics, as many farmers claim, that makes us refuse to pay the higher cost of getting good tomatoes to market? Everyone complains, but still those suspect tomatoes continue to sell. The commercial tomato market racks up an annual sales figure of about $4 billion, despite about a 30 percent drop-off in sales during the winter.

How did this happen? How did we get to this sorry state of inferior abundance and scarce quality? Will it change? What can we do? To find answers, it is helpful to know our tomato's history.

What Is a Tomato?

A tomato is the fruit of the tomato plant, a vine that in its wild state is robust and hearty, a resilient perennial that can grow as tall as a telephone pole or as wide as a row of Cadillacs and has an indefinite life span. Because the tomato develops from an ovary, it is, scientifically, a fruit, although we think of it as a vegetable, which is how it functions on our table—in salads, soups, and main courses, in savory sauces and side dishes. Only occasionally, and with very limited success, does the tomato turn up in desserts. Thus it is functionally a vegetable, and legally, too, as the Supreme Court affirmed in a well-known 1893 decision (see sidebar).

The tomato plant is a member of the nightshade, or Solanaceae, family, making it a cousin of the eggplant, the red pepper, the potato, the ground cherry, the tomatillo, and the highly toxic belladonna,

also known as deadly nightshade. All tomatoes belong to the genus *Lycopersicon*, meaning "wolf peach," and those that we eat are limited, with a few exceptions, to cultivars of one species, *L. esculentum*; the tiny currant tomato, increasingly popular these days, belongs to the species *L. pimpinellifolium*. The wild cherry tomato, the most likely ancestor of our cultivated tomatoes, is *L. esculentum* var. *cerasiforme*, cultivars of which are grown on a very limited basis.

The fruits of the tomato plant grow in a variety of shapes, but each is made up of smooth, satiny skin surrounding meaty flesh that softens as the tomato ripens, with pockets known as locules filled with seeds enveloped by a thick gel. A well-grown tomato is always tart and always sweet, both in varying degrees, depending on the specific variety, climate, method of cultivation, and time of harvest. Tomatoes that are left to ripen on the vine

All about Tomatoes   **5**

have a higher percentage of sugar than do those that are picked green, which fail to develop their full flavor.

Although tomatoes vary greatly in appearance, their actual genetic differences are minute, attributable to a very limited number of genes. On a molecular level, all cultivated tomatoes are remarkably alike. Most of the differences in taste can be attributed to techniques of growing, though certain varieties have individual, if subtle, characteristics.

For culinary purposes, the primary distinctions between tomatoes are size, color, and texture, with each category better suited to certain types of culinary uses than others. Currant tomatoes, tiny little jewels that are either red or yellow, are best eaten right off the vine or used as garnish. Cherry tomatoes—which come in a wide spectrum of colors from white, pink, and pale yellow to bright orange, deep red, and green—are best raw in salads and salsas, grilled on skewers, or cooked simply as a side dish. Certain varieties of cherry tomatoes—the larger ones that have a low percentage of water—make delicious dried tomatoes. Plum tomatoes, with several varieties in various colors, are well suited for sauces, soups, stews, jams, and chutneys, and, because of their dense flesh, for drying. Slicing tomatoes include everything from the intensely flavored Stupice, about two to two and a half inches in diameter, to the often enormous beefsteak and ox heart tomatoes, heirloom varieties currently enjoying a renaissance. Though ideal for their stated purpose, slicing, they also play their part in salsas, sauces, and soups quite well, although they frequently need draining or longer cooking because of their high water content. As specialty growers revive heirloom varieties, obtained through specialty seed catalogs and seed exchanges, tomatoes with unique characteristics have become readily available, like the Valencia, a deep-orange slicer that holds its shape when it is cooked, and the Yellow Ruffle, a nearly hollow tomato that doesn't offer much taste but is ideal for stuffing. The increasingly common Green Grape cherry tomato, green when ripe, is delicious. Unlike their earliest relatives, which were largely ignored or shunned as food, tomatoes today have endless, delicious uses.

The First Tomato

The tomato is a native of the New World, specifically of the South American tropics. Sometime long ago in a fertile river valley in the region now claimed primarily by Peru and Bolivia, a low green vine stretched itself out over the arid land, tumbled over rocks, wove itself between tree and shrub, and reached downward toward the sea. Flowers bloomed on our inaugural vine and gave way to tiny green berry-like fruit, the first tomatoes. Perhaps that primordial fruit was plucked off by an early ancestor; more likely, it shriveled on the vine until its dry skin burst and its seeds scattered on the hot wind.

Today, the progeny of that first tomato plant thrive throughout the Andean region, and some survive under extremely harsh conditions, pushing themselves up like weeds, which they were once considered, through cracks in concrete and frequently thriving with little water in nearly desert-like conditions. Human encroachment has had little impact. The tomato has staying power, as its lengthy struggle for culinary acceptance reveals.

The original ancestors had primarily green fruit—only three wild species show any color—whose size ranged from that of a small pea to that of today's cherry tomato, which is a direct descendant of the fruit of those early types. Although the wild species are not toxic—birds and animals feed on them—their complex taste, according to tomato geneticist Professor Charles Rick, is extremely distasteful to most people. Some have a high sugar content, but the flavors are unpleasant and persist in the mouth.

All wild species of the genus *Lycopersicon* can be traced to the Andean region, yet there is no archeological evidence to suggest that the tomato was widely used as a food or that it was domesticated by the native inhabitants. There is no word for the tomato in the languages of the region, no images of them, and no preserved remains, as is the case with other plants that were used as food. Further, there is no evidence of native large-fruited varieties, which were the first to appear in Europe. For clues about the tomato's early cultivation, we must look to Mexico.

The Tomato's Early Journey

In an article in *Scientific American*, Charles Rick explains that there is greater similarity between older European cultivars of tomatoes and the wild plants of Mexico than between the European varieties and wildings of the Andean region. Woodcuts in early European herbals show large-fruit tomato plants, further strengthening the case for domestication before arrival in the Old World.

Unfortunately, early records of the New World rarely mention the tomato, making the story of the tomato's initial journey ultimately conjecture, based on inference rather than fact. However, we do know the source of its modern name. *Xitomatl*, the undisputed origin of tomato, is from Nahuatl, the language of the Nahua, a group of Mexican and other Central American Indian tribes, including the Aztecs. The tomato had to have moved north to be so named.

The timing is right, too. Cortés took Mexico City in 1519. The tomato makes its first appearance of record, though not by name, in 1544 in an herbal written by Petrus Andreas Matthiolus of Italy, who also reports that the tomato "is eaten in Italy with oil, salt, and pepper." Enough time is thus allowed for Atlantic transport from Mexico, European cultivation, and acceptance as food. Regardless of this initial, simple appreciation, it would take several more centuries before the tomato claimed its rightful place as an indispensable element of the kitchen.

Although the first mention of the tomato is in an Italian publication, there is considerable evidence that it arrived in Europe by way of Seville, Spain, which dominated New World trade in the sixteenth century. The Spanish adopted the Nahuatl name, calling the fruit *tomate*, but the tomato did not enjoy immediate popularity in the country. The first published Spanish recipe (see sidebar, page 11) appears in the seventeenth century, after both the Italian reference and a full chapter in a 1554 publication by Dutchman Rembert Dodoens.

The tomato's name has generated substantial speculation, and it is frequently assumed that the Italian designation is derived from *pomo d'oro*, or "golden apple," which would indicate that the first imported tomato seeds produced yellow fruit. However, in an essay in the *Journal of Gastronomy*, the late Rudolf Grewe, a culinary historian, suggests an alternative explanation involving the eggplant, a close relative of the tomato. Popular among Arabs, the eggplant, Grewe speculates, became known as the "apple of the Moors," or *pomo del moro* in Italian and *pomme des mours* in French. Both terms easily could have been shortened colloquially to *pomodoro* and *pomme d'amour*. Because of their biological similarities, described in the Matthiolus herbal in 1544, it is not far-fetched to imagine early tomatoes being thought of as varieties of eggplant, and the name thus bestowed on the new fruit. This would explain, Grewe continues, the genesis of both the French and the Italian terms, providing a plausible reason that the tomato became known in France as "the apple of love," or *pomme d'amour*.

The Love Apple Makes Its Mark

From today's vantage point of the phenomenal popularity of tomatoes, it is hard to understand why it was so slow to capture the world's culinary imagination. But slow it was. Today, tomatoes are so abundant that their use gives new meaning to the name Red Sea. Just consider how much sauce is spread on pizza skins in a single year in the United States. A red sea, indeed, and that's just one use. Currently, the United States alone produces fourteen to fifteen million tons of tomatoes each year. What took so long?

Although the tomato was eaten in Italy in the mid-1500s, it would be another couple of centuries before it secured its place in cuisines of the southern Mediterranean, where it remains essential today. Elsewhere throughout Europe, it would take even longer, and the tomato had to be reintroduced to the New World by Europeans—Puritans, no less, who brought it in as an ornamental plant—for the United States to be interested.

A statement by herbalist Matthias de L'Obel in 1581 was typical of the early difficulty experienced by the tomato: "These apples were eaten by some Italians like melons, but the strong stinking smell gives one sufficient notice how unhealthful and evil they are to eat." Malignant and poisonous, it was said, with no benefits for human nutrition.

Initially, the tomato was grown largely as an ornamental, its edible fruit treated with frivolous disregard. Myths about its pernicious and indeed

---

Tomato Sauce, Spanish Style

Take half a dozen tomatoes that are ripe, and put them to roast in the embers, and when they are scorched, remove the skin diligently, and mince them finely with a knife. Add onions, minced finely, to discretion; hot chili peppers, also minced finely; and thyme in a small amount. After mixing everything together, adjust it with a little salt, oil, and vinegar. It is a very tasty sauce, both for boiled dishes or anything else.

—Antonio Latini, *Lo scalco alla moderna*,
vol. 1 (1692), trans. Rudolf Grewe

deadly qualities persisted with great tenacity. Certainly, its relationship to poisonous members of the nightshade family didn't help, and perhaps that is the reason it was thought to be toxic. The tomato was approached timidly, with suspicion and uncertainty. If it wasn't poisonous, as surely must have been discovered—if not widely believed—fairly early, then it was an aphrodisiac, an attribute perhaps linked to its name and one that would overshadow its culinary benefits, for better and for worse.

Before its fruit became a popular food, the tomato plant was examined for any possible medicinal effects, and it was found that an alkaloid, tomatine, present primarily in the leaves, was beneficial in treating fungal diseases of the skin. Plants high in this alkaloid show resistance to fungi, an immunity that apparently can be passed on. It was also considered effective against scabies and arthritis, benefits that have not been confirmed in modern times. In fact, consumption of members of the nightshade family can make the symptoms of arthritis worse.

The tomato makes its first written appearance in the United States in an herbal published in 1710, a full seventy-two years before Thomas Jefferson makes the next reference to it. Always the sophisticate when it came to things culinary, Jefferson continues to acknowledge both the horticultural and culinary possibilities of "tomatas" in the Monticello garden book that he maintained from 1809 to 1814.

Clearly, by the nineteenth century tomatoes were gaining wide acceptance and limited but increasing appreciation. They were being grown as a food crop, and their name began appearing in association with ketchup, traditionally made with such ingredients as walnuts and mushrooms. By the 1850s numerous varieties of tomato plants were available from seed salesmen.

Although the tomato continued to be scorned in publications such as the *Boston Globe* as late as 1845, by 1847 Robert Buist in *The Family Kitchen Gardener* claimed that "it is on every table from July to October." Also that year the commercial processing of tomatoes began at Lafayette College in Easton, Pennsylvania. It was the chief gardener at the college, Harrison

Woodhull Crosby, who spawned the tomato-canning industry. He soldered lids on tin pails, leaving a hole on top into which he stuffed whole tomatoes. Next, he soldered a small tin plate over the hole, and then sterilized the tins in boiling water. By 1914, the tomato processing industry was enjoying great success, with thousands of bushels of tomatoes used to produce not only simple canned tomatoes, but soups, ketchup, and chili sauce as well.

In 1994 the Campbell Soup Company celebrated its 125th anniversary. It was the tomato that got this company started in 1869 in Camden, New Jersey. The famous—some would say infamous—Campbell's Condensed Tomato Soup spawned an industry, and by 1990 the company had produced twenty billion cans of it. Today, Campbell's remains committed to tomato research and improvement. Currently, its focus is largely on the nutritional possibilities of the golden tomato. Golden tomatoes are higher in beta-carotene (see page 37) than red ones, and new golden varieties may eventually contain 100 percent of the recommended intake of vitamin A.

Along the way from scorn and obscurity to praise and prominence, the tomato has had its heroes, both real and mythical. Tomato folklore includes the largely fictional account of Robert Gibbon Johnson, who is said to have eaten a tomato—allegedly, the first consumed in this country—on the steps of the courthouse in Salem, New Jersey, in August 1820, thus promoting the safety of the fruit. A look into the actual history of the tomato, the town, and the man does not support this fanciful tale of the tomato in America, but it is a good story. An Ohio seed salesman, Alexander W. Livingston (1821–1898), is honored in the annual Reynoldsburg Tomato Festival, founded in 1973, for his efforts in dispelling the myth of tomatoes as poisonous. And today, of course, there are scientists like the esteemed Charles Rick, who is known casually as Mr. Tomato, a high compliment in today's world.

Growing Tomatoes

Because tomatoes are easy to grow and because those from home gardens almost always taste better than those grown anywhere else at

Mr. Tomato: A Portrait of Charley Rick, the Father of Tomato Genetics

Several months out of the year, the tomato makes up about 50 percent of Professor Charles Rick's diet. His favorite recipe is simple enough: he makes a sandwich using toasted heavy bread, mayonnaise, tomato slices, basil vinegar, salt, and pepper.

"I eat it all the time and never get tired of it," he says, an illustrative answer to my inquiry about how he feels about eating tomatoes after five decades of studying them. Not only does he eat tomatoes with enthusiasm, he grows them in his backyard and makes his own dried tomatoes, using a Cuisinart for slicing and a forced-air dehydrator with temperature control for drying.

Rick, professor emeritus in the Vegetable Crops Department at the University of California at Davis, has devoted his entire professional life to the study of tomatoes, and he remains an unfettered enthusiast. As a young faculty member in 1940, he didn't start out with a passionate interest in *Lycopersicon*, but rather spent his first years studying the asparagus, with an emphasis on gender determination. One day after he'd been on the faculty a couple of years, an older professor commented that it might be interesting to look at a common phenomenon out in the tomato fields: about one plant in a thousand failed to set fruit. Rick thought it sounded boring and initially dismissed the suggestion, saying to himself, "Better to know why they set fruit."

He remembers that about a month later he woke up in a cold sweat, thinking, "You fool, you'd better look at this." Awake the rest of the night, he spent the next day gathering field samples and the remainder of the season studying the fruitlessness of certain tomato plants. He uncovered a multitude of fascinating details, information that led to years of study and a remarkable body of knowledge.

The discoveries Rick made that season proved to be extremely useful, not just in studying the tomato and eventually developing improved varieties, but in mapping the genome as well. The chromosomal maps of the tomato are among the best of any flowering plant. By the 1950s, Rick was aware of the wild relatives of the contemporary cultivated tomato, and he began spending his sabbaticals in the Andes, collecting specimens and studying habitat. It was this crucial research that was partly responsible for the vast number of disease-resistant varieties available to growers, both commercial and casual, today.

Over more than five decades at UC Davis, Charley Rick oversaw the Tomato Genetics Resource Center, which catalogs and stores the seeds of about 3,000 types of tomato plants, including around 4,000 wild species, subspecies, and varieties. Each year it is necessary to replenish the library seed stock of about 300 varieties, a project Rick also administered.

all, a tremendous amount of support and information is available to the home gardener, the result of all of the research, experience, knowledge, and enthusiasm that has accumulated for decades (see Resources and Bibliography, pages 310–312). There exists an entire subculture of backyard tomato growers who pursue their passion with great gusto and dedication and who make their considerable knowledge easily available to aficionados. Whether it is recommendations for seeds for hundreds of varieties with every imaginable characteristic or solutions to every problem from a short growing season to soil nematodes, information abounds that will get you from cultivation of a garden patch to bushels of great tomatoes without much trouble. Growing great tomatoes in your backyard is largely a matter of a few simple techniques and a lot of trial and error as you determine which varieties work best in your particular environment and what, if any, special considerations might be needed.

It is important to understand the basic requirements of the tomato plant before setting out to grow one. Although not temperamental, the plant has specific needs, with different varieties being better suited to certain environments. Tomatoes require at least eight hours of sunlight a day, so if you live in an area where the season is short, consider one of the early-fruiting varieties. There are several, from the well-known Early Girl to numerous heirloom varieties. If you have only a tiny spot on a fire escape in Manhattan, you can get varieties ideal for container cultivation. Temperatures under fifty degrees for more than the briefest periods will damage both fruit and plant, so again, consider your environment before planting. A company in

All about Tomatoes

Northern California offers individual solar greenhouses, small plastic tents filled with water, that enable growers in cooler climates to start their tomato plants several weeks earlier than normal, but if cold nights linger into June, you need to choose varieties with the shortest production time.

Tomatoes don't do well in sustained temperatures much over ninety degrees, though they thrive on heat, and an occasional sizzler won't hurt them. But in areas with particularly hot summers, such as southern Florida, it is impossible to grow good tomatoes during the summer months. Likewise, tomatoes do not do well in high humidity. The plants become prey to all sorts of fungal diseases and nearly always need to be treated with fungicides. Certain varieties have been developed to set fruit in cooler weather, such as the San Francisco Fog, and these varieties are said to do better in hotter weather, too. It appears their temperature tolerance has been stretched in both directions.

Tomatoes need a proper chemical balance in the soil, with nitrogen available in moderate but not abundant amounts. Too much nitrogen and you will have bushy tomato trees without fruit; too little, and the fruit will be puny. In addition to nitrogen, tomato plants need a mix of phosphorus, potassium, sulfur, calcium, magnesium, iron, zinc, molybdenum, manganese, boron, and chlorine. The most efficient way to ensure that all of these minerals are available to your plants is by using good compost or organic fertilizers such as bat guano and blood meal. Should deficient soil be your problem, consult an expert on how to nourish it.

Tomatoes can become easily waterlogged and require good drainage. Careful watering techniques are crucial; too much or too little water causes a plant a great deal of stress. Certainly, plants must be irrigated in dry weather, but in optimum conditions, water can be withheld entirely during the last stages of maturity. Tomatoes that are watered appropriately have better texture and more intense flavor than their overwatered relatives.

Because diseases can pose a severe problem, several experts recommend growing varieties that have had resistance, especially to the common VFN (verticillium wilt, fusarium wilt, and soil nemotodes), bred into them.

Nonresistant heirloom varieties are somewhat trickier to grow, but many gardeners find the gamble worth it; the harvest is diverse, colorful, unusual, and delicious. Nearly all seed packages will state whether a variety has VFN resistance or not.

The best way to find great tomatoes, if in fact you can't grow them, is to spot them in your neighbor's yard or to have a friend nearby who grows them, so be on the lookout. Of course, if that is not possible, look for the best commercial sources, especially the farmers markets now available in most urban as well as suburban areas.

Varieties of Tomatoes

You hear a lot about tomato varieties these days. Heirloom tomatoes have become extremely fashionable and are available not just to industrious gardeners but to eager eaters who frequent farmers markets. Restaurants, too, are in on the designer-tomato trend; many buy specialty tomatoes directly from farmers. This is a real boon to tomato lovers, who have a greater variety available to them currently than they have had in several decades.

With a few notable exceptions, we generally do not know the names of the tomatoes we buy in supermarkets. Although everyone talks about varieties of tomato by name, the vast majority of tomatoes, certainly nearly all commercial stock, are not named at all, but instead identified by numbers. A farmer wanting to grow a tomato with certain qualities can contact the University of California at Davis and choose from thousands of varieties. These tomatoes make their way into cans and onto produce shelves without ever being identified by such charming names as their heirloom cousins sport, such as Charlie's Pride & Joy, Super Sioux, Heart-Shaped Brandywine, and Egyptian Tomb, to mention just a few. A handful of named varieties have made their way into our common vernacular and we find them easily in seed packets, in six-packs of tomato starters at our local nursery, or in the produce bins of a few good markets. The most common of these are Sweet 100, Early Girl, Shady Lady, Celebrity, Better

Boy, Best Boy, Roma, Red Currant, Yellow Taxi, Yellow Pear, Green Grape, Zebra Stripe, Marvel Stripe, and Brandywine.

If you are intrigued by the prospect of growing heirloom tomatoes, several resources are available to you. One of the best is Seed Savers Exchange in Decorah, Iowa. This seed-preservation organization publishes an annual yearbook with thousands of listings of varieties of plants from apples, barley, beans, and corn to flax, millet, onions, and tomatoes. Each variety listed is grown by at least one member of Seed Savers Exchange; a few seeds are available directly from that member for a small fee. Descriptions of each variety list qualities—good and bad—and occasionally historical trivia as well. The book not only offers an enormous amount of information, but is filled with a great deal of charm, too.

Tomato Cultivars for Gardens and Small Farms

This is a sampling of a few of the thousands of tomato varieties available to home gardeners and small farmers. (The type designation—currant, cherry, paste, slicer, beefsteak, and stuffer—refers to the size, shape, or texture of the tomato and should not be confused with varieties of the same or similar names.)

Variety	Type	Characteristics	Best Uses
Ruby Pearl	Red currant	Tiny, very sweet	Garnishes, salads
Broad Ripple Yellow	Yellow currant	True currant, early to ripen, prolific, very sweet, dime-sized fruit	Garnishes, salads
Sweet 100	Red cherry	Hybrid, intensely sweet and juicy, abundant yield	Salads, salsas, grilling
Sun Gold	Orange cherry	Richly colored with intense, distinctive flavor	Salads, salsas, grilling, drying
Green Grape	Green cherry	Large, with lots of flavor and good strong acid	Salads, salsas, and other fresh sauces
Pink Teardrop	Pink cherry	Pale pink, with a musky flavor	Salads, salsas, and other fresh sauces

Variety	Type	Characteristics	Best Uses
Camp Joy	Red cherry	Size of a Ping-Pong ball, excellent flavor	Drying
Yellow Pear	Yellow cherry	Beautiful, yellow, pear-shaped, sweet	Salads, salsas
Snow White	Yellow cherry	Ruffled, pale yellow with white interior, musky flavor	Salads, salsas, delicate sauces
Tiger Tom	Striped cherry	Red fruit with golden stripes, size of golf ball, very tasty	Salads, salsas, and other fresh sauces
Roma	Red paste	Good flavor, high yield, meaty, best canning tomato	Canning, sauces, ketchup, drying
San Marzano	Red paste	Meaty, mild	Canning, sauces, ketchup, drying
Orange Roma	Orange paste	Brightly colored, mild-tasting fruit, low acid	Canning, sauces, ketchup, drying
Yellow Plum	Yellow paste	Meaty fruit, good sweet flavor, prolific	Sauces, jams, ketchup, slicing, salads
Rocky	Red paste	Red fruit with fantastic flavor, sweet and meaty	Slicing, canning, sauces, ketchup, drying
Enchantment	Red paste	Egg-shaped, wonderful fresh taste	Slicing, canning, sauces, drying
Banana Legs	Yellow paste	Shaped like a Roma with a bump on the end, mushy, poor flavor	Novelty appearance is only appeal
Early Girl	Red slicer	Very popular early tomato, small, great true tomato taste	Salads, sandwiches, salsas and other fresh sauces, roasting
Stupice	Red slicer	Small red with outstanding flavor, fine in heat but adapts to cool climates with short seasons	Salads, sandwiches, salsas and other fresh sauces, roasting
Dona	Red slicer	French hybrid, easy and reliable to grow, great true tomato flavor	Salads, sandwiches, salsas and other fresh sauces, roasting
San Francisco Fog	Red slicer	Medium red with good temperature tolerance and good taste	Sandwiches, salsas, and other fresh sauces

All about Tomatoes

Variety	Type	Characteristics	Best Uses
Valencia	Orange slicer	Firm orange flesh, few seeds, retains shape when cooked, can be difficult to grow	Stir-fry, chutneys, salsas, and other fresh sauces
Peach	Yellow slicer	Pale yellow fruit with an apricot blush, fuzzy, delicate subtle flavor	Slicing, salads, sandwiches
Taxi	Yellow slicer	Medium-sized bright yellow fruit, wonderful old-fashioned flavor	Slicing, salads, sandwiches, salsas, and other fresh sauces
Great White	White slicer	Slight melon flavor	Delicate sauces such as vinaigrettes, salads
White Wonder	White slicer	Ivory-colored with a pale yellow blush, good taste	Delicate sauces such as vinaigrettes, salads
Green Zebra	Green slicer	Small tomato with yellowish stripes	Slicing, salsas, and other fresh sauces
Red Rose	Red beefsteak	Large red fruit, great flavor, cross between Brandywine and Rutgers	Slicing, grilling, summer soups
Evergreen	Green beefsteak	Large, bright green flesh, great flavor	Slicing, salads, gazpacho, salsas, and other fresh sauces
Caro Rich	Orange beefsteak	Large deep-orange fruit, low in acid, high in beta-carotene, sweet and mild	Gazpacho, slicing, salsas, and other fresh sauces
Brandywine	Dark red beefsteak	Large, old-time tomato flavor	Gazpucho, slicing, salsas, and other fresh sauces
Marvel Stripe	Marbled beefsteak	Flesh is marbled yellow and red, very large, full of good flavor	Slicing, salads, salsas, and other fresh sauces
Black Krim	Dark beefsteak	Large Russian tomato, dark reddish brown or purple, green shoulders, unique, full-bodied flavor	Slicing, salads, sandwiches, grilling
Yellow Ruffle	Yellow stuffer	Nearly hollow yellow tomato with minimal flavor	Stuffing

Sources: Seed Savers Exchange, Johnny's Selected Seeds, Dragonfly Farms, Grand-View Farms

Preserving the Harvest

In the days when we all lived closer to the land, it was common practice to pull up the last of the tomato plants—those still heavy with green fruit—by their roots and hang them, upside down, on the walls of the root cellar, the pantry, or, in the proper climate, a protected back porch. The tomatoes would ripen slowly, stretching out the season for a few more precious weeks. There is no reason this can't be done today and I am sure it still is, though fewer of us have our own tomato plants, and even fewer have a root cellar or a pantry large enough to accommodate a bush or two on the wall. Should you be blessed with both land and space, give it a try, being sure to sort through the branches every few days and pluck off not just the ripe fruit but any that may have spoiled. Plants hung in this fashion are particularly vulnerable to insects, and so you must pay close attention to protect your bounty.

There are alternatives to this most romantic of tomato preservation techniques. If you have two or three days to set aside at the peak of harvest, you can make it through the winter with a pantry stocked with wonderful preserved tomatoes. If you have a garden, perhaps you already preserve the essence of the tomato season in jars, bottles, and freezer bags. But you don't have to grow your own tomatoes to take advantage of their season. At the height of the harvest, an abundance of tomatoes must be dealt with pronto, before the rotting process sets in. It's neither difficult nor expensive to purchase a few lugs to put up for the cooler months.

These days, you can even make your own dried tomatoes easily with a forced-air dehydrator. For cooking, the best tomatoes to dry with this handy machine are Romas, with their thick, meaty flesh and low percentage of water. For snacking, however, both cherry tomatoes and slicing tomatoes—cut very thin—are delightfully sweet and tangy. They are also beautiful, especially when you use multicolored tomatoes, like Marvel Stripe. Dehydrators come with instructions for drying a variety of fruits and vegetables.

Tomatoes take well to freezing as long as they are sealed in airtight packages and used within about three months. Simply peel them, remove the stem end, and freeze them whole or coarsely chopped. Of course, frozen tomatoes cannot be used to replace fresh ones, but they are fine for soups and sauces. Most tomato sauces can be frozen, too; just pack them in conveniently sized containers.

Finally, putting up tomatoes—a somewhat more laborious task than drying or freezing—is a great way to spend a couple of days in the dead of summer (see Preserving Tomatoes, pages 279–285, for specific techniques and recipes). You might begin by reading about others who do it. *On Persephone's Island* by Mary Taylor Simetti includes a wonderfully evocative account of the long tradition of making tomato sauce in Sicily.

Commercial Tomatoes

California dominates the commercial tomato industry, with 90 percent of the nation's tomato crop coming from the Golden State, where the arid conditions most closely mirror the tomato's original environment. California's typical lack of rainfall from April through October is ideal for tomatoes, which suffer from too much moisture. Although California could produce outstanding tomatoes, and does so on a limited basis, the majority of the crop is tasteless—grown to bounce, as one detractor puts it. Seventy percent of tomatoes for fresh sales are picked at the mature green stage, well before the natural sugars and acids have had time to develop. They are reddened with the application of ethylene gas. "Vine-ripened" tomatoes, which represent 30 percent of the market, are picked at the breaker, or turning, stage and have only the barest hint of color. These tomatoes generally are left to ripen on their own, without being gassed, though their full flavors fail to develop once they are removed from the vine.

Although there are a number of specialty growers in the state who offer a great variety of true vine-ripened tomatoes, production is very low,

> Making the year's supply of tomato sauce is the most important domestic ritual in the Sicilian summer, and each housewife believes in the efficacy of her favorite method with fervor equal to that with which she believes in the efficacy of her favorite saint. There are basically two rival schools of thought: the one favors passing the scalded tomatoes through the tomato mill, then sterilizing the filled and capped bottles in boiling water; the other prefers to heat up the empty bottles, fill them with boiling hot tomato sauce, and then lay them in a nest of woolen blankets, so well wrapped that they will take several days to cool off.
>
> —Mary Taylor Simetti, *On Persephone's Island*

forming barely a fraction of the commercial tomato industry. Still, good tomatoes are there to be had by the lucky or diligent shopper.

Even sunny California has an off-season, which spans from the first winter frost, generally sometime in October though occasionally as early as mid-September, until the beginning of the next year's harvest, during which time Florida and Mexico play important roles in the fresh tomato industry. Florida dominates the market, with Mexico frequently offering fierce competition. Florida production drops off as summer approaches; the temperatures are simply too high for the tomato to thrive. Fungal diseases are also a problem in Florida, where the high humidity encourages their growth. Nearly all Florida tomatoes are treated with fungicides.

Setting aside the consideration of taste just momentarily, the strides made by the tomato industry in the last several decades are astonishing. Yields have increased significantly as acreage devoted to commercial tomato production actually has decreased, owing largely to the pioneering work of Professor Charles Rick. Forty years ago, California's yield was approximately 13.5 metric tons of tomatoes per hectare; today it is over fifty. Rick's research with the ancient wild tomatoes of the Andes has resulted in new varieties that are resistant to diseases once capable of decimating entire crops and has opened up areas to cultivation where tomatoes once

All about Tomatoes

failed to thrive. The soil nematode, for example, made it impossible to grow tomatoes in certain soils until scientists developed a variety immune to the nematodes. But in spite of these advances, corporate agribusiness, both in California and elsewhere, faces numerous problems—from the overuse of chemical pesticides and fertilizers and lack of crop rotation to the mistreatment of migrant farm workers and the cultivation of foods for maximum profit rather than for taste and nutritional value. These issues are best discussed elsewhere, but it is important to keep them in mind when considering the shortcomings of commercial tomatoes.

Commercial Tomato Products

Like tomatoes grown for general commercial distribution, tomatoes used to produce the many products on our shelves, from simple canned whole tomatoes to chili sauce, ketchup, soups, and stews, are from determinate vines, plants with fruit that ripens all at the same time. This allows for mechanical harvesting and gets an entire field of tomatoes picked and to the processor quickly. Unlike tomatoes grown for fresh distribution, tomatoes for processing can and generally do remain on the vine until both their color and their flavor develop—they are usually picked at the light red stage, when their sugar and acid levels are high—which is the primary reason that canned tomatoes tend to be far superior, even in the summer months, to standard commercial tomatoes. In winter and spring, there is no comparison between canned tomato products and commercial fresh tomatoes.

Several varieties of tomatoes are used for commercial canning and rarely is the variety named. Rather, it is chosen from among hundreds of numbered varieties, sought for specific qualities such as high sugar, low water, high yield, good flavor, and disease resistance. In addition, growers seek tomatoes with specific traits that allow them to thrive in particular soils and climates.

For many years, canned tomatoes imported from Italy were said to be superior to domestic brands. These imports were generally known as San Marzano, a popular variety of Roma tomato named for a specific region near Naples that has traditionally grown them in great number, and the designation was enough to sell them over other brands, even though the name often specified simply San Marzano style. The reputation of San Marzano tomatoes remained steady through the mid-1980s, with noted cookbook authors and food editors indicating these tomatoes in their recipes. Several taste tests, including those whose results appear in *Cooks Illustrated* (March/April 1994) and Jennifer Harvey Lang's *Tastings* reveal a reversal in this trend. Although *Cooks Illustrated* blames higher tariffs for the decline in Italian tomato products—the assumption being that it is no longer profitable to pack them for export—several importers offer another explanation. Certainly, the imposition of a 100 percent tariff on imported tomatoes makes them less attractive than their California equivalents, but the quality has decreased as well. Industrial pollution is a severe problem and areas that once produced vast quantities of high-quality tomatoes have been adversely affected, not only in their yield, but also in the quality of their product.

Currently, a few brands coming from Italy offer excellent-quality tomatoes, but it is no longer safe to assume that the choice of an import—which is usually two to three times more expensive than its domestic equivalent—ensures quality. I frequently use Pomi tomatoes, a brand distributed by Parmalat USA Corporation, which are packed in small boxes rather than cans. I find they offer dependable taste and texture. I also use the San Marzano tomatoes imported by Taste of the World (Morristown, New Jersey) when I can find them.

Tomatoes of the Future

There are two general trends in the commercial tomato market. The movement toward organic products is immensely important, and best represented currently by Muir Glen, a company based in Sacramento, California, that is producing high-quality tomato products from organically grown fruit. The other significant development comes to us from nearby, in the university town of Davis just south of Sacramento, where a snappy

young biotech firm, Calgene, Inc., is working to place tomatoes with true backyard flavor into every supermarket in America.

Although Muir Glen is neither the first nor the only producer of organic canned tomatoes—Eden Foods launched its organic crushed tomatoes in 1990—its aggressive marketing plan and beautiful, bold packaging have brought dramatically increased awareness of the availability of organic tomato products. A division of the large Sierra Quality Canners, Muir Glen is producing canned whole tomatoes, ground tomatoes, diced tomatoes, tomato juice, tomato sauce, tomato paste, and several other tomato products from organically grown tomatoes. Founded in 1991, the company that was named in honor of the great nineteenth-century environmentalist John Muir has doubled its production each year.

Muir Glen contracts directly with organic farmers throughout California's Central Valley to grow tomatoes to its specification. After harvest, the tomatoess are trucked to Sierra Quality Canners' facility in Gilroy for processing. Muir Glen's tomatoes are packed in lead-free steel containers that have been coated with white enamel to eliminate the slight metallic taste of many canned tomato products. Interestingly, in both casual and formal taste tests, many consumers have shown a preference for tomatoes that have picked up a bit of taste from the can, a fact that underscores the power of sensory memory. Many dishes based on canned tomatoes are comfort foods; that longing for the foods of youth will be satisfied by the same flavors, the faint taste of metal included. Increasingly, though, people are coming to realize the benefits—both to themselves and to the environment—of organic products. And those who make the switch to organic tomatoes without metallic residue will raise a generation who seek their unadulterated flavor.

The other trend in commercial tomato production in the early 1990s involved fresh fruit and was basically a challenge to the tomato's perishable nature. In the natural world, tomatoes left on the vine until their flavor is fully developed have a short post-harvest life, four or five days at

Timber Crest Farms

Imagine a tomato field at midnight, cloaked not in a quiet cape of darkness but lit by bright halogen lamps and teeming with activity. Huge truck-trailers pull in to receive their loads of juicy red fruit and take off into the cover of night, winding their way to the heart of the wine country, to Dry Creek Valley in Healdsburg, California, where some of the state's finest grapes are grown. Here you will also find Timber Crest Farms and its resident tomato visionary, Ruth Waltenspiel, the woman who single-handedly created the American dried-tomato industry. Every night throughout California's tomato harvest, trucks snake their way from the north Central Valley toward this small town in northern Sonoma County so that at the crack of dawn the work can begin. The tomatoes are floated out of the trucks and trailers on a bath of cool, clean water. They go through several additional rinses before they are sorted, cut in half, set on racks, and wheeled into huge dryers, from which they will emerge a few hours later to again be sorted and sent on their way either to storage or for additional processing as dried-tomato bits, dried tomatoes marinated in olive oil, or the other Sonoma-brand dried-tomato products of Timber Crest Farms.

All this began in 1979, when Ruth Waltenspiel returned home from a gourmet-food show determined to compete with the high-priced sun-dried tomatoes imported from Italy and then just becoming popular among trendy eaters. She was allowed two truckloads. Processing went beautifully on the first load, and when at about 2.00 a.m. the tomatoes seemed to be drying beautifully, she turned off the heaters and the fans that had previously dried only the fruits that she and her husband produced. She went to bed. An early morning phone call brought the news of green mold, and that was the end of the first truckload of dried tomatoes, which ended up in the orchard as compost. The next truckload was more successful, and Timber Crest Farms was on its way to creating a domestic dried-tomato industry. In 1993 the farm processed 913 truck and trailer loads of tomatoes, or over seven million pounds of Roma tomatoes. Timber Crest Farms remains the leader in the industry.

The Waltenspiels have since sold their business but Sonoma-brand dried-tomato products continue to thrive under new ownership.

All about Tomatoes

most. That's plenty of time to get a crop of tomatoes to the processor for canning, but getting fresh tomatoes to the marketplace poses a much greater challenge. Calgene, a company based in Davis, had been working since 1982 to develop a technique that would add time to a tomato's post-harvest life, thus allowing it to ripen on the vine and still make it to markets far from the field. In 1994, the company appeared to have succeeded; that spring, Calgene won approval from the Food and Drug Administration for the new designer tomato. In early summer, the tomato was introduced in a few limited regions of California and Illinois, and initial sales were phenomenal, far beyond Calgene's projections. Yet success eluded the engineered tomato.

The FlavrSavr, or MacGregor, tomato, as Calgene's creation has been named, was the first genetically engineered product to be offered for retail sale, and the process sparked no small controversy. To grasp the issues, we must understand how the tomato was created. A gene in all tomatoes triggers the production of an enzyme that degrades pectin, causing the tomatoes to soften, the initial stage in the process of rotting, which begins soon after ripe fruit is picked. Because ripe tomatoes are highly perishable, allowing little time for them to be picked, packed, shipped, unloaded, displayed, and sold to consumers all over the country, most tomatoes are picked at the mature green stage.

After identifying the gene that triggers the release of the pectin-hungry enzyme, Calgene scientists cloned the gene, reversed it, and reinserted it into the tomato so that it gives a negative, or antisense, message. The process of pectin degradation is stalled and the life of a ripe tomato is extended by at least fourteen days. At this point, the altered tomato contains only its own DNA—albeit altered, but its own nonetheless. Calgene was issued a patent on this process, antisense RNA technology that covers its function not just in the FlavrSavr tomato, but in a broad range of plants. The technology enables a partial or complete inhibition of specific plant functions.

In order to identify those plants that have undergone successful gene reversal—the insertion of the altered gene doesn't always work—a marker gene is attached to the side of the reversed gene. This marker gene, which comes from a naturally occurring bacterium, creates an immunity to kanamycin, the antibiotic present in the test medium in which Calgene's tomatoes are grown. The FlavrSavr seeds were resistant to the drug and thrived; those without the reversed gene, and thus without immunity, died or failed to thrive adequately. Calgene could therefore identify the FlavrSavr tomato without waiting for harvest and then setting tomatoes on a shelf and watching them rot.

Calgene bought time with its high-tech engineering. The antisense gene allowed the tomatoes to ripen on the vine and extended their post-harvest life so that they could make it to markets around the country with time to spare. The specific function of the altered gene appears benign; it is the marker gene and its resistance to antibiotics that is the lightning rod for objections to the tomato.

In the end, the MacGregor tomato was a commercial failure, floundering in the marketplace and vanishing into obscurity soon after Monsanto purchased Calgene, Inc., in 1996. It's a good thing. The more we know about GMOs, the less appealing and the more dangerous they appear.

Tim Hartz, head of vegetable crop production at UC Davis, scoffs at most of the opponents of genetic engineering, comparing them to those who have resisted everything from Galileo's view of the solar system to the invention of the loom. But he is not a strong advocate of the designer tomato, regarding it as a high-tech solution to a problem that could be easily solved without advanced genetics. He sees some irony in the situation when he explains that vine-ripened tomatoes could be available 365 days a year. The reason they aren't is that consumers so far have been unwilling to pay the higher price they must command. Post-harvest costs soar for vine-ripened fruit because they must be handled more carefully and get to market more quickly. Hartz suspects that once farmers see that consumers are willing to pay a premium price for the engineered tomato, they will be eager to compete for a share of the ripe-tomato market. He predicts the appearance of better-quality tomatoes in the major markets, a tomato war of sorts fought not only in lab petri dishes, but also in the fields of old-fashioned, low-tech farmers who may finally be able to engineer a profit out of vine-ripened tomatoes.

Tomatoes and Health

Although, with one exception, a single tomato is not remarkably high in any particular nutrient, we eat such a substantial quantity—currently about eighty pounds per person annually—that they provide a larger percentage of dietary nutrients than any other fruit or vegetable. A tomato doesn't even make it into the top ten when it comes to nutrient concentration (the top spots go to broccoli, spinach, Brussels sprouts, lima beans, peas, asparagus, artichokes, cauliflower, sweet potatoes, and carrots, in that order); the tomato

Tasting the Fruits of Biotechnology

I arrived at Calgene, Inc., early one morning and was led into an employees' lunchroom, where Carolyn Hayworth, manager of public relations, handed me a plump red MacGregor tomato with a blue, green, and red sticker over the stem end. The tomato was heavy in my hand; it was deeply colored and had a ripe feeling. *It is an attractive tomato*, I thought to myself, in spite of a few yellow blemishes Hayworth apologized for. The spots didn't bother me; in fact, they made me feel more comfortable. *It's real*, I thought as I turned it in my palm. *It is not a monster.* Of course, blemished fruit such as the one I held will be discarded before it gets to market. Customer resistance to such flaws is much higher than resistance to pesticides, herbicides, or genetic engineering. Interestingly, statistics show greater consumer concern about the safety of organic products than about that of genetically altered ones.

I sliced the MacGregor tomato in half, noticing the pleasant way it yielded to the knife. It fell open to reveal deep red flesh, plenty of it, and small, tightly packed seed pockets. It glistened invitingly and a faint tomato aroma beckoned. It looked as though it would make a good gazpacho. Did I hesitate a moment before slicing off a piece? Was I wary of the marker gene, afraid I might be violating some natural sanctity of body that was hitherto pristine, untouched, a biogenetic virgin? Frankly, no, my brazenness stemming perhaps from the fact that I am a child of the '60s, a member of a generation with a long history of chemical experimentation. Why stop now?

I followed my first bite with a second, and then a third, considering flavor, texture, acidity, balance, and finish. I added a little salt to one bite, cut pieces in different shapes, and tried those. The tomato was slightly sweet and had a pleasantly silky texture, plenty of tomato flavor, and just a bit of characteristic acid. There was no getting around it; this was a damn good tomato, not the best I've ever tasted but far better than anything I've ever gotten in a supermarket.

I finished every last bit of my first MacGregor tomato and headed home, stopping at a nearby supermarket, where I picked out a tomato that sat under a "Garden Fresh" sign. The tomato was hard in my hand but not particularly heavy. It was the same pale pinkish red as all the other tomatoes in the large pile. I brought it home and cut into it: it didn't give under the knife at all. The inside flesh was hard and the seed pockets were large and full of runny liquid. There was no aroma. I sliced off a piece and took a nibble. Tasteless, except for a sharp bite of acidity. If this, the supermarket tomato, is MacGregor's competition, I know where I'd place my bet.

comes in at sixteen, just after cabbage and before bananas, but we eat so many of them that they top the chart when it comes to their contribution to our diet. (Nutrient-rich broccoli, spinach, and Brussels sprouts are twenty-one, eighteen, and thirty-four, respectively.)

A tomato is made up mostly of water, but so are we. The tomato's nutrients include vitamin A and a substantial amount of vitamin C (about 32 percent of the Recommended Dietary Allowance), trace amounts of several other vitamins, a bit of iron and other minerals, a little fiber, and a very small amount of protein. Like all fruits and vegetables, the tomato does contain a smidgen of fat but, of course, no cholesterol, and delivers a mere five calories per ounce, or about thirty calories in an average slicer.

Because the tomato contains vitamin A, it also contains one of its precursors, beta-carotene, which recently has become a buzzword because it is thought to lower the risk of cancer. It is now suspected that it is not only beta-carotene that offers cancer protection but also its cousins, the carotenoids. Among these relatives is one called lycopene, and the tomato—whether fresh or as tomato sauce, juice, or paste—contains more of it than any other produce (almost twice as much as second-ranking watermelon). The tomato, in fact, is the star of this particular show because it surpasses all other vegetables and fruits in total carotenoids, since over two-thirds of them come from lycopene, news that should encourage you to freely indulge. When you consider how much taste is packed into a single good tomato, it's a real nutritional bargain.

Charley Rick told me the story of hearing of a man who claimed he lived exclusively on tomatoes. A wealthy man with food allergies, he traveled continuously, following tomato season. A nutritionist confirmed that the fellow's interestingly limited diet was possible, but added that he probably took a protein supplement. Most people can eat tomatoes with abandon, particularly if they do so without the addition of ingredients that alter the tomato's benign nutritional profile. Although allergies to the tomato itself are said to be rare, the pollen and the tiny hairs on the stems and foliage of the plant can cause a skin rash in some people. Additionally, there is substantial evidence that members of the nightshade family (potatoes, eggplants, tomatoes, peppers) aggravate the symptoms of rheumatoid arthritis, though without any apparent lasting effect or damage.

Tomatoes in the Kitchen

Nearly all kitchens in America have tomatoes in various forms in their cupboards and pantries. Whether it is a bowl brimming over with a rainbow of heirloom tomatoes or a cupboard stocked with ketchup and pasta sauce, we

find tomatoes nearly everywhere that people cook, or simply eat. Even college students are likely to have a bottle of ketchup or a frozen pizza slathered with tomato sauce stashed away. The tomato serves us well, but with a bit of knowledge, this culinary workhorse will perform even more successfully.

When working with fresh tomatoes, the most important quality to understand is the effect of temperature. Their flavor begins to deteriorate when the thermometer drops below about fifty-four degrees Fahrenheit. So don't refrigerate your tomatoes. It is certainly tempting, especially as the harvest gets into full swing, to extend the life of all those extra tomatoes by chilling them. Unfortunately, it renders them tasteless and makes the flesh mealy. Try to use fresh tomatoes within three to four days, and if you can't, make a simple sauce or salsa that will hold in the refrigerator for a few extra days.

When it comes to the problematic half tomato, there is no satisfying answer. If it sits at room temperature, it will spoil rapidly. If you refrigerate it, it will lose its flavor. Why not just eat it? If you simply can't, chop it coarsely, cover it with either olive oil or vinegar, and use it the next day in a salad dressing or sauce.

When it comes to cooking with fresh tomatoes, the guidelines are equally simple. To retain that bright, fresh flavor, cook tomatoes quickly. If they're cooked longer than about thirty minutes, their flavor begins to change as sugars are released and liquid evaporates. The resulting taste can be insipid. To transform this quality, tomatoes must undergo lengthy, slow cooking, a technique that applies to just a few recipes such as a traditional ragù. So the rule here is to cook tomatoes for a very short time or, on occasion—primarily when meat is an ingredient—for a very long time.

When should you peel tomatoes, and how? Any tomato with troublesome skin—too thick, scarred, or otherwise damaged—should be peeled, as should tomatoes for most sauces and for canning. For quick sauces and salsas, especially uncooked ones, it is up to you. Some people prefer their tomatoes peeled; others like that bit of resistance the skin

All about Tomatoes   **39**

offers. The same is true for tomatoes to be used in salads, though more people accept the skins here than in sauces. A peeled tomato is silkier and more elegant than an unpeeled one; let that quality be your guide. If a friend serves me a platter of sliced tomatoes from his garden, I expect that they will have their skins and that is fine with me.

To seed a fresh tomato, peeled or unpeeled, is simple. Cut it in half horizontally—that is, through its equator—hold each half over a bowl, cut side down, and gently squeeze out the seeds and gel, coaxing them out with your finger if necessary.

If you find you have particularly watery tomatoes on hand, seed them, chop them coarsely, and then place them in a strainer and let them drain for ten to fifteen minutes. The addition of a bit of salt will speed up the release of water, but it is not absolutely necessary.

To purée fresh or canned tomatoes, use a food mill rather than a food processor or blender. In one step, you will get a smooth, dense purée with the seeds and skins removed. A blender or processor will make the tomato foamy because it introduces air into the purée.

The guidelines for cooking with canned tomatoes are similar to the rules for working with the fresh fruit. It does not take long to make a simple, flavorful sauce or soup from good-quality canned tomatoes. To make a rich, meaty sauce with great depth of flavor, lengthy cooking over extremely low heat is necessary. Reliable recipes will recommend suitable cooking times, but be skeptical of those that call for an hour or so of simmering. That is too long for lighter sauces, yet doesn't allow enough time for the development of richer flavors.

Like fresh tomatoes, canned whole tomatoes should have their stem ends and seeds removed. This can be done quickly with a small, sharp knife or with your fingers; I prefer my fingers. Simply pull away the hard stem end and squeeze out the seeds and discard them. Passing the tomatoes through a food mill is an efficient way to separate the seeds, though the ends must be removed and the tomatoes broken up by hand first.

How to Peel a Tomato

Beware! Books and articles that tell you to plunge a tomato into a pot of boiling water for thirty to sixty seconds are wrong. Left in its bath for more than fifteen seconds, your tomato will cook. This is simply common sense.

But a water bath is not a good way to peel a tomato, no matter how briefly you leave it. This too is simply common sense: the water dilutes the flavor.

The best way to peel one or many tomatoes is to scorch the skin over a gas flame or hot burner. To do this, skewer a tomato through its stem end with a dinner fork. Hold it in the flame or close to the burner and rotate it as the skins sears and pops. It takes about five to fifteen seconds per tomato, depending on size. The heat will intensify the taste of the tomato. *Do not put tomatoes in a cold water bath to cool them; it will only further dilute the flavor.* Simply let the tomatoes cool slightly and then use your fingers to pull off the skins. A well-grown, properly ripened tomato may not need the extra help; its skin should pull off easily with a sharp knife, though the process is a little slower than the direct-flame method. To encourage the skin to loosen, rub the tomato with the dull edge of a knife and then peel it. You may also peel certain varieties of tomatoes—firm-fleshed Romas, for example—using a standard vegetable peeler.

When using canned tomatoes, it is important to know your ingredients. Not all canned tomato products are of equal quality. Indeed, I find a great deal of variation, particularly among canned whole tomatoes. Many are mushy; some have a thin and insipid taste with slightly metallic undertones; others are overly acidic or too sweet. The amount of tomatoes per can varies a great deal, too: some have as few as seven or eight tomatoes; others have a dozen or more. The best way to discover the brand of canned tomatoes that works for you is to taste all that are available in your area and choose those that you like.

Tasting Tomatoes

The best way to learn about any food is to taste it. Whether you are trying to find a great olive oil, a good mustard, a perfect peach, or your

favorite tomato, nothing substitutes for the immediate experience upon your palate. Of course, informed tasting is ideal, but knowledge cannot be substituted for direct experience. Certainly, it is important to have an intellectual understanding of the food in question, a knowledge of its ideal properties. Armed with these factual details, set out to find the fresh tomatoes and canned products that you like best.

In the culinary classes I teach at our local college, I give my students an assignment in comparative tomato tasting, and I am always astonished by the number of people for whom such an experience is a revelation. So many people have given up on the possibility of finding good-tasting tomatoes; they are resigned to the mealy commercial tomatoes sold year-round in supermarkets, forgetting that just off the main road are neighbors and farmers offering the real thing. Because the course is offered in the fall during the peak of the tomato harvest, a comparative tasting works perfectly. The students fill out their tasting forms for each of the tomatoes they've gathered—one from a major market, one from a legitimate farm stand or market, one from a home garden—and write an essay about the exercise. For the younger students, all too many of whom have been raised on a diet of fast food, the assignment can be transformative. It is often the first time they have tasted a "real" tomato. For older students, the exercise often brings back memories of tomatoes

To Fix a Thin Sauce

Although a sauce made primarily of tomato paste is too thick and unpleasantly cloying, tomato paste is ideal for rescuing a sauce or salsa that is too thin; it will add structure to such mixtures. To correct a thin sauce, stir in a teaspoon or two of double-concentrated tomato paste (available in convenient tubes), tasting after each addition, until you have achieved the consistency you seek. This technique works with fresh, uncooked salsas as well as with cooked tomato sauces and soups. Just guard against adding too much paste or your sauce will take on its characteristics rather than retain the original recipe's flavors. I recommend no more than two teaspoons per cup of sauce.

eaten as children, which is frequently the last time they tasted a tomato with backyard flavor. The exercise changes nearly all students' buying—and eating—habits.

Tasting a variety of tomatoes can offer a great deal of pleasure. Unlike certain organized tastings—olive oil, for example, or vinegar—a fresh-tomato tasting does not involve eating a food out of its normal context. Many people recoil at the idea of tasting a spoonful of oil or sucking on a sugar cube soaked in tart vinegar, but nearly everyone can appreciate the pleasure of a bite of tomato. The purpose of tasting tomatoes in this formal manner is to familiarize yourself with the particular characteristics of certain varieties. Because texture—and thus, shape—plays an essential role in how foods taste, I recommend tasting both slices and pieces of each tomato. Consider nuance of flavor, texture, and aroma, and be sure to pay attention to the tomato's color and the thickness of its skin. Commercially grown tomatoes often have thick, unpleasant skins; the skins of boutique tomatoes are generally thinner and more delicate, easy and pleasant to eat. After you taste a slice and a spoonful of diced tomatoes, add a little salt to a piece and see how that influences the flavor. A bit of salt on a fresh, raw tomato is essential, drawing out flavors on the tongue that might be missed without it. At the conclusion of the tasting, toss the remaining tomatoes together as a salsa, salad, or fresh tomato sauce.

Consider tasting commercial canned tomatoes with a group of friends who share an interest in cooking. This way, several people can explore the various qualities and discover those brands they prefer. And afterward, of course, the leftover tomatoes can be made into a sauce and you can end your tasting with a spaghetti lunch or dinner.

Taste in an organized fashion. After displaying the products to be tasted in the manner described in the tasting menus (pages 46–47), assess the tomatoes visually, one brand at a time, considering their color and consistency. Is the liquid surrounding the tomatoes thin and watery? Do the tomatoes appear to be mealy? Are the stem ends hard and green, or is

The Kendall-Jackson Tomato Tent

Two years after the first edition of this book was published, Kendall-Jackson Winery in Fulton, California, in central Sonoma County, launched a tomato festival that featured a handful of chefs offering their tomato specialties, an art show, and live music. It was small and homey, a lovely way to spend an afternoon in late September. It grew like a tomato on steroids and draws thousands of visitors each year. And throughout the growing season, the winery sells the more than a hundred varieties of tomatoes—both as plant starters in the spring and tomatoes in the summer—it grows at this location and a farm in nearby Alexander Valley.

In 2015, the winery will host the 19th Annual Heirloom Tomato Festival, which has grown into an enormous event, with dozens of chefs ringing a huge grassy field. A high point of the festival is the tasting tent, where more than a hundred varieties of tomatoes from the winery's extensive gardens are offered for tasting. There is a growers competition, with three divisions, one for cherry and currant tomatoes, one for the heaviest tomato, and one for slicers that includes four subcategories: white and green; yellow and orange; pink and red; purple-brown and black. A Best of Show Tomato is selected from the winners in divisions one, two, and three.

Prizes are awarded to food vendors, too. In 2014, Applewood Inn & Restaurant in Guerneville took the Critic's Choice prize for its rabbit sausage corn dog with heirloom tomato ketchup.

The festival also includes a chef competition, workshops, music, and tomato-inspired surprises. In 2003, I organized the World's Biggest BLT, with a parade of ingredients, costumed mascots—lettuce, tomatoes, and salt flakes—and, best of all, a Mayo Queen.

When the Mayo Queen dropped her golden spatula and commanded, "Let the slathering begin!" thirteen teams spread the mayonnaise, tiled the tomatoes, sprinkled on the salt, stacked the bacon, crowned it with lettuce, and, all at once, added the 103 feet of bread on top. Completion took less than fifteen minutes and then we sliced and sold the sandwich, which was every bit as good as we hoped it would be. I've since recreated the sandwich, both larger and smaller versions, with more to come because, really, who can resist a giant BLT?

the entire tomato a rich, ripe red? Are there blemishes or black spots? Note your reactions on the evaluation form before continuing.

Next, spoon a portion of the tomato product into your bowl, leaning close to catch the aroma. Does it smell fresh? Finally, taste the product, considering both texture and flavor. Is it silky, watery, mealy, oily? Does it taste like fresh tomatoes? Is there a bitter or metallic aftertaste? Is it too sweet or too acidic? Note all of these reactions on the evaluation form and then continue until you have evaluated all the brands of tomatoes. Discuss your reactions with the other tasters, and retain the information for reference.

Menus for a Tomato Tasting

Fresh Tomatoes

For each taster:
A small bowl of kosher (coarse-grain) salt
A small glass plate and a fork
A large glass of water
An evaluation sheet (see Tasting Notes, page 298) and a pencil
A napkin

For the table:
One each (for cherry or currant tomatoes, a cluster) of up to twelve varieties of fresh tomatoes, either all of a similar type or all of a specific common quality (all cherry tomatoes, all orange tomatoes, all tomatoes from a single garden, and so on), left whole

A glass plate displaying the same tomatoes sliced, placed in front of their corresponding whole tomatoes (cut cherry tomatoes and pear tomatoes in half)

A glass bowl displaying the same tomatoes cut into half-inch dice, placed in front of their corresponding whole tomatoes (this step is unnecessary for cherry tomatoes)

Pitchers of water

For Canned and Other Commercial Tomato Products

For each taster:

Several small glass bowls
One or two plastic spoons
Several unseasoned water crackers
A large glass of water
An evaluation sheet (see Tasting Notes, page 298) and a pencil
A napkin

For the table:

Up to eight similar tomato products (all canned whole tomatoes, for
    example) in their containers
Glass bowls filled with the products to be tasted, set in front of their
    corresponding containers
Large serving spoons for each product to be tasted
Pitchers of water
A basket of unseasoned water crackers

PART 2
The Annotated Tomato Pantry

A Well-Stocked Tomato Pantry

Any cook needs a good supply of tomato products in the pantry, not just for carefully planned menus and favorite recipes, but for those culinary emergencies that inevitably occur: unanticipated guests, a busy schedule, a sudden craving for spaghetti, an unexpected storm. With a shelf full of good canned tomatoes and just a few other ingredients, you can put together a quick meal without much effort. And often simply adding a small amount of tomato—a tablespoon or two of tomato paste, for example, or a squeeze of dried tomato purée in a tube—is just what a bland soup or sauce needs to perk it right up.

I think it is best to avoid commercial tomato products with additional ingredients—currently, you can find everything from basil leaves and garlic to Cajun spices, chipotles, and roasted peppers—as they limit your options and, more importantly, frequently have a strong chemical taste. Wholesome organic tomatoes with nothing more than salt and, sometimes, citric acid, give you the best options for adding your own seasonings.

These are the products that I find essential, unless you put up tomatoes from your own garden.

For the reluctant cook:

Ground (or crushed) tomatoes:
Perfect for a quick soup or spaghetti sauce

Tomato sauce:
Essential in many simple soups and sauces

Double-concentrated tomato paste in a tube:
Much less troublesome than a can of tomato paste—half of which invariably goes to waste—and so easy to use.

The culinary enthusiast will want the basics, along with these products:

Canned tomatoes:
Whole in juice, diced, chopped, ground or crushed, strained, sauce, double-concentrated paste

Dried tomatoes:
Marinated dried tomatoes, dried-tomato purée in a tube, dried-tomato bits

A Glossary of Commercial Tomato Products and Traditional Tomato Sauces

Although home cooks have been making sauces in their kitchens for centuries and will continue to do so without ever opening a book, certain sauces have long traditions, and a mere mention of their names can conjure up their subtle flavors.

All'Amatriciana Traditional spicy tomato sauce for pasta, made with onions, pancetta, tomatoes, and hot peppers.

Andalouse A velouté (white sauce made with chicken stock, veal stock, or fish fumet) seasoned with concentrated tomato purée, sweet peppers, and parsley.

Arrabbiata Another charmingly named, traditional Italian tomato sauce, this one from the south. The name translates literally as "anger" or "rage," which refers to the substantial amount of red pepper flakes that characterize this pasta sauce.

Aurorea Velouté seasoned with concentrated tomato purée.

Bolognese See Ragù

Choron A classic Béarnaise sauce (a reduction of herbs, aromatics, wine, and vinegar emulsified with egg yolk and butter) flavored with concentrated tomato purée.

Concassé A condiment of fresh, uncooked tomatoes that have been peeled, seeded, and finely chopped. It is seasoned simply, generally only with salt, and forms the basis of other sauces.

Coulis The term once referred to sauces and gravies in general; today a tomato coulis is a simple but intensely flavored reduction of fresh peeled and seeded tomato pulp that has been drained of its liquid and cooked briefly in butter or olive oil with garlic and herbs.

Double-Concentrated Tomato Paste A reduction of tomato paste; thick and intensely flavored. Italian versions available in tubes are convenient to use in small amounts and keep well in the refrigerator.

Dried-Tomato Bits Commercial dried tomatoes that have been ground into small pieces; useful in vinaigrette, risotto, polenta, and in any recipe where uniform distribution of dried tomatoes is important.

Dried-Tomato Purée Dried tomatoes that have been reconstituted, puréed, and seasoned with herbs and olive oil; intensely flavored and convenient to use in a variety of recipes.

Dried Tomatoes Tomatoes that have had their water extracted through exposure to dry heat; intensely flavored with a slightly leathery, chewy texture.

Fondue A classic sauce of peeled, seeded, and chopped tomatoes, pressed through a sieve and cooked in butter until soft. It may contain various seasonings such as garlic, herbs, sweet pepper, and paprika.

Ketchup The classic sweet condiment ubiquitous in the United States, where it is served automatically with hamburgers and french fries. Today, to be called ketchup a product must contain tomatoes, vinegar, and sugar; it must be labeled "artificial" if the sugar is omitted. Most ketchup also contains onions, salt, and spices (most commonly allspice, black pepper, cinnamon, cassia, cloves, cayenne pepper, ginger, mustard, and paprika). In Europe, the condiment was traditionally made with mushrooms or walnuts, but the sauce is thought to be of Chinese origin.

Marinara The familiar quickly cooked tomato sauce seasoned with garlic and onions. Some sources say the name—literally, "of the sailors"—refers specifically to sailors coming into port in Naples with Italy's first tomatoes; others say it refers to the speed of preparation, suitable to sailors who were in a hurry to get back to work.

Nantua A velouté made with fish fumet and flavored with either fresh tomatoes or tomato purée.

Portugaise Sauce espagnole (classic brown sauce; one of the three "grand sauces" in classical cuisine) with ripe tomatoes, garlic, olive oil, and tomato sauce.

Puttanesca A spicy Italian sauce with capers, black olives, anchovies, oregano, garlic, and tomatoes. Translated literally, the name means "in the style of the whores."

Ragù Meat sauce from Bologna, frequently called Bolognese sauce; the richest of the classic tomato sauces. Marcella Hazan recommends three essential steps in making successful, authentic ragù: the meat must not be browned, merely cooked long enough to lose raw color; the meat must be cooked in milk before tomatoes are added; and the sauce must simmer as slowly as possible for a minimum of three and a half hours; five is better, she says.

Salsa Although the word translates literally as "sauce," salsa is used to designate variations of a spicy condiment of Mexico—traditionally, a mixture of tomatoes, onions, chilies, and cilantro. Today a "salsa" can be made with everything from chopped mangos to diced clams and roasted coconut, the word indicating that the mixture has some level of heat and is a condiment. In Italian cuisine, "salsa" simply means sauce (as in, say, salsa alla Marinara). With all of the cultural crossover today, there is occasional confusion.

Stewed Tomatoes Chunks of tomatoes seasoned with a variety of herbs and spices; commercially, one of the most popular canned tomato products in the United States.

Sun-Dried Tomatoes Tomatoes that have been sliced and set in the hot sun long enough, generally two to three days, for their water to evaporate. Although these are virtually unavailable commercially, many products on the shelf, as well as recipe and menu items, read "sun-dried tomatoes." Chances are, they are not.

Tomato Paste Legally, the liquid obtained from mature red tomatoes or from the residue of tomatoes prepared for canning or juice. The liquid is concentrated, may be treated with both hydrochloric acid and sodium hydroxide, and can be seasoned with salt, spices, flavorings, or baking soda. The label must indicate these additions. Salt and basil are the two most common additions.

Tomato Purée The liquid obtained from mature red tomatoes or from the residue of tomatoes prepared for canning or juice. The liquid is concentrated, but not to the degree that tomato paste is.

Tomato Sauce Tomato purée to which seasonings—especially salt, pepper, dried garlic, and dried onions—have been added.

PART 3
A Tomato Cookbook

Cooking with Tomatoes

What is a recipe, truly, if not an invitation? "Here is where I've gone," the cook who offers up a recipe says. "I liked it here and I think you will, too." From this perspective, a recipe is not simply a list of ingredients and a few instructions; it is a call to adventure, mapped by a fellow explorer who made the journey before you or who found a slightly different way of getting there. Certainly, following the recipes here to the letter will yield results worthy of the good ingredients you choose. But you also should use the recipes for inspiration, as I do when I curl up in bed at night with a cookbook rather than a novel. Let my ideas, my ways of enjoying the tomatoes that I love so thoroughly, inspire your own.

The recipes you find here are a mix of tradition and innovation. Some are my interpretations of classic recipes that have been with us for decades and longer, adjusted to suit my palate, my cooking style, and the ingredients at hand. Others have been inspired by my environment, by the fact that I live in a virtual Garden of Eden when it comes to all things agricultural. There is an almost daunting supply of wonderful ingredients in California's Sonoma County, which provide a constant source of inspiration and renewal. From sometime in June or July through the end of October and now and then into November, tomatoes of every shape and color are in glorious abundance. The recipes featuring fresh tomatoes are a result of this bounty and the creativity it ignites.

The most important thing to keep in mind when working with these—or any other—recipes is to seek the best ingredients available. Treated with care and intelligence, a fine tomato is difficult to damage. Taking the time to find the highest-quality foods will give you the best results.

A Note about Organization

In this edition, I have eliminated the Main Course/Entrée category, as, honestly, that's not really how I think of tomatoes. A tomato, no matter how extraordinarily delicious, is rarely at the center of the plate, no matter the meal. As I wrote, it began to seem a tad gymnastic to break things into the usual category of appetizers, soups, salads, pastas, main courses, side dishes and basic recipes. One of the primary ways we enjoy tomatoes at dinner is in some sort of pasta and many of the best pasta dishes use classic sauces in a variety of ways. These recipes are collected in the chapter on sauces, with suggestions for use following each recipe. Many of my soups are ideal as main courses, as are salads, egg dishes, and vegetable dishes. Organize your meal, whether breakfast, brunch, lunch, dinner, or midnight snack, around what is fresh where you live and don't worry about the traditional hunk of protein surrounded by a couple of side dishes that has long been the default version of dinner in America.

To Grind or to Blend, That Is the Question

Grind, I always say, by hand.

Beginning in the 1950s, electrical appliances became fashionable. Mechanical tools were replaced, and while I doubt many regret that the electric mixer supplanted the handheld rotary beater, many useful tools disappeared in favor of new inventions. For example, the potato ricer—which looks a little like an oversized garlic press—all but vanished, even though it gives a fluffy, uniform texture to cooked potatoes that is impossible to achieve by other means. The food mill, too, was nearly completely discarded.

Both have been rediscovered and are now readily available almost anywhere cookware is sold.

The food mill is a simple machine with a handle, a large bowl with changeable blades, and a paddle with a central hand crank, typically connected by a screw fitted with a wire on the underside that turns close to the bowl, scraping off the purée as the paddle presses it through the

Essential Tomato Tips

Once you have great tomatoes, it is important to know how to handle them so that they retain as much flavor and as pleasing a texture as possible.

- Do not store fresh tomatoes in the refrigerator; cool temperatures degrade a tomato's texture, turning it mealy.

- Store tomatoes, stem end down, on a platter large enough to hold the tomatoes without them touching. Keep the platter away from heat and light, in a cool part of the kitchen, pantry, or dining room. Use them within three days or within two days if they are very ripe or if the weather is particularly hot.

- If you have more tomatoes than you can use, chop them, stir in a little olive oil, and keep them in the refrigerator, covered, for a day or two.

- To peel a fresh tomato, *do not* plunge it into boiling water, as most cookbook authors and chefs suggest. This process cooks up to a quarter-inch of the tomato's outer flesh and it dilutes the flavor. Instead, insert a fork into the stem end of a tomato and hold it over a hot flame, burner, or coals. Turn it fairly quickly so that the skin pops and begins to blister. Set aside for a minute or two to cool and then use your fingers to peel off the skin.

- If you love tomatoes, invest in a good tomato knife, available at local cutlery stores.

- For sliced tomatoes, always cut parallel to their equators. For wedges, cut from pole to pole.

- To remove a tomato's gel and seeds, slice it through its equator and hold it, cut side down, over a bowl. Squeeze gently and, if necessary, use a finger to loosen the gel.

- To make a salsa or simple sauce, put chopped tomatoes into a strainer set over a bowl to drain for several minutes, stirring from time to time as they drain. Save the juices—sometimes called tomato water—to make a simple chilled consommé seasoned with lemon juice, olive oil, and salt or to make a summer Bloody Mary.

A Tomato Cookbook **59**

bowl's small holes. Mills have broad legs, so to speak, that rest on the container that will catch the purée. The machine comes apart for easy cleaning and is simple to reassemble. Food mills are inexpensive—the best are under $50—simple to clean, and easy to store. And if there's a power failure, you won't be left with a half-made sauce.

A food mill is essential when making a good tomato sauce. It excludes seeds and skins and, more importantly, purées without creating foam, as blenders and food processors do. Electric grinders incorporate air as they operate and the foam is an unavoidable and *always* unwelcome by-product of the process. With just a few exceptions, do not purée tomatoes in processors or blenders; grind them through a food processor. Blenders and processors incorporate air as they operate, which is fine for certain food, emulsions, for example, but dreadful for most vegetable or fruit-based sauces. If you love to cook, invest in a food mill.

A Note about Salt

All the recipes in this book were tested using flake salt, either Diamond Crystal Kosher Salt, Maldon Sea Salt Flakes, or Murray River Flake Salt. I recommend salting in stages, as you go, so that you build in flavor, rather than salting at the end of cooking. You will typically use less salt when you add it in this way. I typically don't give specific quantities, as I think it is best to salt to taste and to use your fingers and not a measuring spoon to add it.

If, for whatever reason, you omit salt from these recipes I cannot guarantee the final outcome, as salt makes flavors blossom. I've always thought of it as flavor's midwife; without it, recipes are often stillborn.

Salt is a lifelong passion for me and I explore it in detail in *The Good Cook's Book of Salt & Pepper*, to be published this fall. It is a revised edition of *Salt & Pepper* (Broadway Books, 1999), which I wrote in 1998.

Starters, Nibbles & Snacks

A huge array of tomato dishes make delicious appetizers, especially when you scale them down to bite-sized nibbles. An Insalata Caprese (page 128), for example, becomes perfect finger food when you wrap little mozzarella balls in basil and stuff them into hollowed-out cherry tomatoes or thread the little balls on skewers, alternating with cherry tomatoes.

Serve gazpacho in shot glasses and hot tomato soup in espresso cups, accompanied by tiny grilled cheese sandwiches.

Salsa with chips is a great way to start a meal, as well, especially in the summer when few things are as refreshing as tomato salsa and a cold Mexican beer. Oysters on the half shell drizzled with a little Tomato Mignonette (page 262) is a special fall treat.

Dried tomatoes, especially those you make yourself (page 286) are delicious as snacks, including in children's lunches.

At the height of tomato season, the best appetizer of all may be a simple bowl of Sweet 100s, a golden cherry tomato that is so sweet and so delicious that it is tempting to simply stand next to a plant and gobble them down.

Cherry Tomatoes Filled with Skordalia, with Variations

Tomato Bruschetta

Pan Tomate

Simple Fried Tomatoes with Hot Bread

Polenta Tartlets with Cherry Tomatoes

Lamb & Eggplant Dolmas with Tomato-Lemon Sauce

Striped Tomato Brie

Tomato Granita with Serranos & Cilantro

Cherry Tomatoes Filled
with Skordalia, with Variations

Makes 24 pieces

Stuffed cherry tomatoes make great appetizers, single bites that can be stuffed with any number of delicious things, from guacamole, corn salsa, and tapenade to shrimp salad, steak tartare, and ceviche. My favorite version is probably this one, with rich, voluptuous skordalia, a blend of garlic, olive oil, and potatoes.

Skordalia, recipe follows
24 round cherry tomatoes, of relatively uniform size
24 Chive flowers or Society Garlic flowers

Make the skordalia, cover it, and refrigerate it for at least an hour and as long as overnight.

Shortly before serving the filled tomatoes, slice off the stem end of each tomato, cutting about 1/8 inch down, just before you get to its wide shoulder. Discard the stem end. Use a grapefruit knife or very small spoon to scoop out and discard the seeds. Set the tomatoes, cut side down, on absorbent toweling until ready to fill.

To add the filling, put the skordalia into a pastry bag, and fill each tomato so that there is a peak of skordalia rising out of it. Top with a flower and serve.

Skordalia
Makes about 1 cup

1 russet potato, about 10 to 12 ounces, baked until tender
4 to 5 large garlic cloves, crushed
Kosher salt
1 egg yolk
⅓ to ½ cup best-quality extra–virgin olive oil
1 tablespoon freshly squeezed lemon juice
Black pepper in a mill

While the potato is still quite warm, break it in half and pass it through a potato ricer into a medium bowl. If you do not have a potato ricer, use a soup spoon to press it through a strainer; do not put it into a food processor.

Put the garlic cloves into a suribachi, sprinkle with salt, and use a wooden pestle to grind the garlic into a smooth paste. Add the egg yolk and mix until very smooth. Use a rubber spatula to incorporate the riced potatoes.

Begin to mix in the olive oil, adding just a bit at a time. Continue until the potatoes no longer look dry and have a sort of glistening sheen to them. It may feel like you are adding too much olive oil but you are not. The skordalia should not be the texture of mashed potatoes and should not be dry at all; it should be smooth and voluptuous. Taste and add more salt, if needed; pour the lemon juice over the salt and then mix it in. Season with a few turns of black pepper, cover, and refrigerate at least an hour so that the volatile oils in the garlic soften a bit.

Variations:

- Make the skordalia and set it aside. Prepare a simple salsa using corn kernels from one cob, lightly cooked. Add a minced serrano, a bit of minced red onion, a bit of minced cilantro, a squeeze of lime juice or lemon juice, and salt and pepper to taste. Use a spoon to fill the tomatoes. Spread a generous amount of skordalia on an oblong serving platter, set the filled tomatoes on top, and enjoy right away.

- Omit the skordalia. Make tuna tapenade, spoon or pipe it into the cherry tomatoes, and serve on a bed of Italian parsley sprigs.

- Omit the skordalia. Make your favorite olive tapenade, spoon it into the cherry tomatoes, top each one with a leaf of Italian parsley, and serve right away.

- Omit the skordalia. Fill each tomato with fresh chèvre, old-fashioned cream cheese, or farmers cheese, top with minced fresh herbs, and serve right away with minced fresh Italian parsley or basil.

- Omit the skordalia. Fill each tomato with smashed egg salad (2 hard-cooked eggs, cooled and smashed with a fork, 2 tablespoons mayonnaise, 2 teaspoons Dijon mustard, and salt and pepper to taste).

- Omit the skordalia. Combine about 4 to 6 ounces of crème fraîche with a tablespoon of snipped chives, 2 teaspoons of minced red onion, and salt and pepper to taste. Spoon or pipe the filling into the tomatoes and top with the best caviar you can afford.

Tomato Bruschetta

Serves 6 to 8

Italian by tradition, all manner of bruschetta have become immensely popular in America. It's about time, too, as bruschetta is delicious and one of the best and simplest ways to enjoy fresh tomatoes. On a hot summer night, serve it outside, with flutes of sparkling rosé.

1 loaf country-style bread such as sourdough, or Italian, cut into thick slices
3 ripe beefsteak tomatoes, peeled, seeded, and cut into small dice, or 1 pint
    cherry tomatoes, quartered
2 tablespoons chopped basil, chopped Italian parsley, or snipped chives, optional
Kosher salt
Black pepper in a mill
Several garlic cloves, cut in half
Best-quality extra-virgin olive oil

Grill or toast the bread.

Put the tomatoes into a bowl, add herbs, if using, season with salt and pepper, and set aside.

Rub one side of each piece of toast with garlic and set the bread on a large platter. Spoon tomatoes on top, drizzle with olive oil, and serve right away.

Variations:
- With Anchovies: Drape each slice of bread with an anchovy fillet after rubbing it with garlic.
- With Mozzarella: Top each piece of bread with a slice of mozzarella fresca after rubbing it with garlic.
- For little bruschetta, use a baguette instead of a full-sized loaf.

Pan Tomate
Spanish Tomato Toast

Serves 4 to 6

In restaurants all over northeastern Spain, it is common to find a plate of tomatoes and garlic already on the table when you sit down. After you have placed your order, a basket of toast arrives. Spaniards know what to do—rub the garlic over the bread, do the same with the tomato, season with olive oil and salt—but I've seen Americans eat the tomatoes, and even the whole cloves of garlic, before the waiter even arrives. Oops.

8 to 12 thick slices sourdough or other country-style bread, toasted or
    grilled until golden brown
6 large garlic cloves, unpeeled and cut in half lengthwise
6 small (2-inch-diameter) ripe tomatoes, cut in half through their equators
Best-quality extra-virgin olive oil
Malton Salt Flakes, Sel Gris, Fleur de Sel, or kosher salt.
Black pepper in a mill

Have the bread hot, in a basket and covered with a tea towel.

Put the garlic and tomatoes on a plate, and have the olive oil in a bottle or cruet from which it is easy to pour.

Set a piece of bread on a plate and rub one side of it with the cut side of a half clove of garlic, pressing firmly. Next, rub a piece of tomato into the same side of the bread, pressing firmly so that the pulp of the tomato is deposited on and in the bread. Discard the skins of the garlic and tomatoes.

Drizzle a little olive oil over the bread, and add a generous sprinkling of salt and one or two turns of black pepper.

Eat and repeat.

Simple Fried Tomatoes
with Hot Bread

Serves 4 to 6

I frequently serve this for lunch with friends in the middle of summer, especially when we have the whole day to linger. Something about sopping up the yummy juices with our bread stimulates conversation. It also makes a great side dish.

6 large firm-ripe tomatoes
2 tablespoons butter
2 tablespoons olive oil
3 to 4 garlic cloves, minced
Kosher salt
Black pepper in a mill
2 tablespoons minced fresh herbs (any combination of Italian parsley, chives, basil, thyme, and oregano)
Sourdough hearth bread, sliced and lightly toasted

Slice off the stem end and blossom end of each tomato and either discard them or save these pieces for another use.

Cut the tomatoes into ¼-inch-thick rounds.

Set a large, heavy skillet over medium-high heat, add the butter and olive oil, and, when the mixture is hot, add the garlic; sauté about 90 seconds. Add the tomatoes in a single layer, working in batches as necessary, and cook for 2 minutes. Turn and cook for 2 minutes more. If working in batches, use a spatula to transfer the tomatoes to a platter, leaving behind the pan juices.

When all of the tomatoes have been cooked, pour the pan juices over them.

Season with salt and pepper, scatter the herbs on top, and serve immediately, with the bread alongside for sopping up the juices.

Polenta Tartlets
with Cherry Tomatoes

Makes 24 tartlets

The best way to ensure that the tartlets are easy to remove from their tins is to rinse them with water just before filling them; do not dry them.

½ cup coarse-ground polenta
2 teaspoons kosher salt, plus more to taste
24 small cherry tomatoes, quartered
2 garlic cloves, minced
1 tablespoon extra-virgin olive oil
Black pepper in a mill

2 teaspoons unsalted butter
⅓ cup (about ¾ ounce) freshly grated Parmigiano-Reggiano
½ cup Pistou (page 253), Red Chimichurri (page 251), or Red Chermoula (page 252)

Pour 2½ cups of water into a small saucepan, bring to a boil over high heat, reduce the heat to medium, and slowly add in the polenta, stirring constantly in one direction. Add the salt and stir continuously until the polenta thickens, about 8 to 10 minutes. Reduce the heat to low and cook, stirring frequently, until the polenta is tender, about 15 minutes more.

Meanwhile, put the tomatoes, garlic, and olive oil in a small bowl. Season with salt and several turns of black pepper and toss gently.

When the polenta is tender, stir in the butter and cheese, taste, correct the seasoning, and remove from the heat.

Rinse 24 small muffin tins in cold water; shake off excess water. Divide the tomatoes among the tins, arranging 3 or 4 pieces in the bottom of each. Use a sturdy soup spoon to fill each tin with polenta, pressing it gently into the tin. When all are filled, cover lightly with wax paper or parchment and let set for up to 15 to 20 minutes.

Remove the tartlets from the tins carefully and invert them onto a serving platter so that the tomatoes face upward. Top each tartlet with a small dollop, about ½ teaspoon, of Chimichurri or Chermoula and serve right away.

Lamb & Eggplant Dolmas
with Tomato-Lemon Sauce

Makes about 6 dozen dolmas

Although these dolmas are not, strictly speaking, traditional, they evoke the flavors and aromas of classical Middle Eastern cuisine. I have been making them for decades and they remain one of my favorite appetizers. The tangy tomato-lemon sauce is the element that ties all the flavors together.

Tomato-Lemon Sauce, page 278
1 pound ground lamb
5 cloves garlic, minced
1 medium eggplant, peeled and cut into ½-inch cubes
¾ cup pine nuts, toasted (see Note below)
2 tablespoons chopped fresh mint leaves
2 teaspoons chopped fresh oregano
Kosher salt and freshly ground black pepper
2 8-ounce jars of grape leaves in brine, drained and rinsed

Make the sauce and set it aside.

In a heavy skillet, sauté the lamb, breaking it up with a fork, until it just loses its color but does not brown. Add the garlic and sauté 2 minutes more. Add the eggplant and sauté over low heat until the eggplant is very soft and tender. Remove from the heat and stir in the pine nuts, half the mint, and the oregano. Taste the mixture and season it with a little salt and pepper. The filling and the sauce may be made a day in advance and refrigerated. Remove them from the refrigerator about 30 minutes before using.

To fill the dolmas, place a leaf, dull side up, on your work surface. Put about 2 teaspoons of filling in the center of the leaf. Fold the bottom of the leaf up over the filling and fold the two sides, one after the other, toward the center and over the top of the filling. Roll the bundle up to the tip of the leaf and place it seam side down in a shallow baking pan. Repeat until all the grape leaves have been filled.

Place the dolmas in a shallow baking pan. Ladle the sauce over them and bake them in a 325°F oven for about 20 minutes. Remove them from the oven and garnish them with the remaining chopped mint and, if using, the wedges of preserved lemons from sauce. Serve immediately.

NOTE

It is best not to use pine nuts from China unless you know with absolute certainty that you (and anyone who will be eating with you) do not have a negative response to them. There is a syndrome called "pine mouth" that seems to be caused by two varieties of pine nuts used in China but nowhere else. A day or two after eating Chinese pine nuts, those who are sensitive to them develop a persistent bitter taste that lingers for days, weeks, or months. Because it does not occur immediately, most people do not associate the problem with the pine nuts. It can be quite alarming, especially if it continues for several weeks. Pine nuts from Korea do not cause the problem, nor do pine nuts from Europe and America, though they are hard to find.

Striped Tomato Brie

Serves 6 to 8

This simple appetizer is nice to have around during the holidays or any time when unexpected guests may show up. When you make it, be certain the Brie is not too ripe, as a fully ripened cheese will not hold together for filling and reassembly.

2 round, semi-ripe 8-ounce Brie cheeses, chilled
¾ cup Tomato Butter (page 250), at room temperature
1½ cups toasted walnuts, finely chopped

To cut the chilled Brie in half, you will need a piece of dental floss (waxed is best) about 2 feet long. Set one of the cheeses on your work surface. Wrap the floss around it horizontally, positioning it in the middle of the narrow edge of the cheese. Gather both ends of the floss in your right hand, holding close to the cheese. Use your left hand to keep the cheese steady, and, with your right hand gently pull the dental floss through the cheese, cutting it in half. (Reverse hands if you are left-handed.) Separate the halves, placing them with the cut side up on your work surface.

Cut the second Brie.

On the surface of one side of each of the cheeses, spread the butter about 1/8 inch thick. Top with the second half of each cheese. Spread the outer circumference of each with a thin coating of the butter and then dip the buttered edge in the chopped walnuts so that they stick and form a crust-like coating around the outer edge of the cheese. Serve the cheese immediately with crackers or slices of baguette, or wrap it tightly and store in the refrigerator for up to 5 days or in the freezer for up to 3 weeks. Remove from the refrigerator 30 minutes before serving and from the freezer at least 2 hours beforehand.

Tomato Granita
with Serranos & Cilantro

Serves 8

Serve this luscious tomato ice as an appetizer or between courses to freshen the palate. It adds an elegant touch to a formal dinner party but is also welcome on a hot summer day.

2 pounds ripe red or golden tomatoes, peeled, cored, and seeded
1 or 2 serranos, seeded and minced
3 tablespoons finely minced fresh cilantro
Juice of 1 lime
Pinch of kosher salt
Pinch of sugar
Cilantro sprigs for garnish

Set a food mill over a deep bowl and pass the tomatoes through it.

Add the serranos and lime juice.

Taste the mixture and if it seems bland, season with salt; if it is too acidic, add a pinch or two of sugar.

Pour the liquid into two metal ice-cube trays or one 9-x-13-inch baking dish and place in the freezer for at least 5 hours, until the mixture is frozen solid.

An hour before serving, remove the granita from the freezer, break it into chunks, place it in a food processor, and pulse quickly until the mixture is slushy. Spoon it in individual glass bowls or dishes and return it to the freezer.

To serve, remove from the freezer, set on plates, garnish with cilantro sprigs, and serve immediately.

Alternately, freeze the granita in a commercial ice-cream maker according to the manufacturer's instructions.

Variation:

- For Bloody Mary Granita, season the tomatoes with a shake or two of Worcestershire sauce, a shake or two of Tabasco sauce, ½ teaspoon of celery salt, and a teaspoon or two of prepared horseradish before freezing it. Rub the rims of glass serving bowls with lime and dip into a plate of flake salt. Just before serving, add a jigger of good vodka that you have kept in the freezer over each portion. Garnish with celery leaves and serve immediately.

A Tomato Cookbook   **75**

Soup, Beautiful Soup

Say "tomato soup" and nearly everyone in America instantly envisions the iconic can of Campbell's and very quickly thinks of its classic companion, a grilled cheese sandwich. The combination has been a rainy-day meal, a sickbed lunch, an after-school snack, and even dinner on a lazy night when no one feels like cooking. As a child, I never liked the soup—I preferred Lipton's Noodle Soup—but I am not immune to its classic imagery. And when I am recovering from a flu or cold, it's what I want, though I typically head to a favorite café that makes a style of tomato soup I do like, which is to say one that tastes like tomatoes and isn't sweet, as canned versions typically are.

You can divide homemade tomato soups into two general categories: those made in the summer with ripe tomatoes and those made in the winter with preserved or canned tomatoes. A third category, soups in which tomatoes play a supporting rather than starring role, spans the seasons.

In this chapter, I explore both summer and winter tomato soups but, for the most part, do not address those soups in which tomatoes play a secondary role, as that could embrace, literally, hundreds of recipes from around the world. I chose a few favorites and left it at that.

When it comes to making tomato soup, the same rules apply that apply to any recipes: the results will never be better than the ingredients, so choose the very best tomatoes available.

Cold
Classic American Gazpacho
Gazpacho with Avocado Purée
Salmorejo: Thick Gazpacho from Cordoba
Smoky Gazpacho
Golden Peach Gazpacho
Yogurt and Tomato Soup

Hot

Tomato Cilantro Soup

Tomato Broth with Seed Pasta

Hearty Summer Tomato Soup

Tomato & Potato Soup

Tomato Bread Soup

Summer Shell Bean and Tomato Soup

Tomato & Corn Chowder with Salmon, Ginger & Lemongrass

Thai-Style Chicken Soup with Tomatoes, Coconut Milk & Cilantro

Pasta Fagioli Soup

White Bean, Tomato & Chorizo Soup with Cilantro

Italian-Style Fish Soup with Crab

Tomato & Crab Bisque with Ginger & Golden Caviar

Tomato Stilton Soup with Fried Sage Leaves

Posole Rojo

Seafood Posole

Creamy Tomato Soup in Puff Pastry

Gazpacho & Other Chilled Soups

Today, the soup we call gazpacho is more of a chunky salad suspended in a tomatoey liquid than it is its original Spanish ancestor. The soup arose in the Andalusian region of Spain, as a way to use every last bit of the staples at the heart of the peasant diet: garlic, bread, vinegar, and olive oil. Every fragment of bread, every edible remnant, was used to make this ancient cousin of gazpacho, which was seasoned with vinegar, olive oil, and salt and eaten at room temperature. Today, summer gazpacho remains at least somewhat true to its spiritual roots, as it is an excellent way to use summer's vegetables at the peak of harvest, when it can be hard to keep up with all the tomatoes, cucumbers, and zucchini. And those original foods that gave gazpacho its essential flavor—garlic, vinegar, and olive oil—are as essential today as they were back then.

Contemporary tomato gazpacho is just one of the paths that lead back to its roots. There are many others, some with grapes and almonds or pine nuts, some with raisins and walnuts, some with fresh fruit, others with clam juice, lobster, and almost anything else a chef wants to put into a liquid and serve chilled.

In this section, I focus on classic American gazpacho, along with the variations I have enjoyed and developed over the years. The most important principle, I believe, is to make gazpacho only when tomatoes are in season where or near where you live. It is a summer indulgence.

Classic American Gazpacho

Serves 6 to 8

This full-bodied version of contemporary gazpacho is best at the peak of harvest, when all of the vegetables are dazzlingly ripe. And on a hot day, there is nothing more refreshing. The soup is flexible and you can change it up by omitting the vegetables not at hand and by using lime juice instead of lemon juice if you prefer.

5 or 6 large ripe tomatoes, peeled, seeded, and chopped
1 serrano, minced
5 cloves garlic, minced
2 lemon cucumbers, peeled, seeded, and diced
1 red onion, peeled and thinly sliced
1 firm-ripe avocado, peeled and diced
Kosher salt
4 cups vegetable, chicken, or beef stock
Juice of 1 lemon
2 tablespoons medium-acid red wine vinegar
2 tablespoons chopped fresh basil
2 tablespoons chopped fresh Italian parsley
4 tablespoons chopped fresh cilantro
Black pepper in a mill
Best-quality extra-virgin olive oil

Combine the tomatoes, serrano, garlic, cucumbers, onion, and avocado in a large bowl. Season lightly with salt, cover, and let rest for about 10 minutes.

Stir in the stock, lemon juice, and vinegar and add the basil, parsley, and cilantro. Taste, correct for salt, and season with several turns of black pepper.

Chill the soup, covered, for at least 1 hour.

To serve, ladle into soup bowls, drizzle with olive oil, and enjoy.

Gazpacho
with Avocado Purée

Serves 4 to 6

I typically make this soup with yellow and orange tomatoes, as I love the rich delicacy of those fruits and I love the contrast of color, too. That said, use the best beefsteak variety tomatoes you have.

4 cups Tomato Concassé (page 263), from red or yellow beefsteak tomatoes
3 cups chicken stock
6 garlic cloves, minced
1 small red onion, minced
⅔ cup fresh lime juice, from 4 to 5 limes
Kosher salt
Black pepper in a mill

2 tablespoons minced fresh Italian parsley
1 tablespoon fresh minced chives
1 tablespoon minced fresh cilantro
1 large or 2 small ripe Hass avocados
1 to 2 serranos, stemmed, seeded, and diced
4 tablespoons best-quality extra-virgin olive oil

Put the Tomato Concassé and chicken stock into a large bowl, add the garlic, onion, and ⅓ cup of the lime juice, and stir together thoroughly. Season to taste with salt and pepper and stir in the parsley, chives, and cilantro. Cover and chill for at least 2 hours.

Meanwhile, peel the avocado, remove the pit, and put the avocado into the container of a blender or the work bowl of a food processor fitted with the metal blade. Add the remaining ⅓ cup lime juice, serranos, 1 teaspoon kosher salt, and ½ cup water and blend or process until the mixture is very smooth. Taste and correct the seasoning. Put the avocado purée into a small pitcher with a narrow spout or a squeeze bottle with a medium-sized opening. Chill thoroughly.

To serve, taste the gazpacho, and correct the seasoning. Ladle it into soup bowls, but do not fill them all the way. Beginning at the outer edge of each serving of soup, slowly pour a swirl of avocado purée, ending in the center, into each soup. Drizzle a little olive oil on top and serve immediately.

Salmorejo
Thick Gazpacho from Cordoba

Serves 4 to 6

This soup is very close to what you will find in Cordoba, Spain, though I have added my own flourish in the form of smoked Spanish paprika. For a more traditional version, leave it out. On a hot summer's night, this rich and satisfying soup is all you'll need. On a cool evening, it makes a great first course.

3 to 4 ounces day-old sourdough hearth bread, crusts removed, in chunks
Warm water
1½ pounds ripe dense-fleshed tomatoes, peeled, cored, and seeded
3 garlic cloves, crushed and minced
2 to 3 teaspoons smoked Spanish paprika, optional, to taste
Kosher salt
1 tablespoon sherry vinegar
3 tablespoons extra-virgin olive oil, plus more for drizzling
2 hard-cooked farm eggs, peeled and grated
1 tablespoon minced Italian parsley
Black pepper in a mill
2 ounces jamón serrano, in very thin strips

Put the bread into a bowl, cover with warm water, and set aside for 15 to 20 minutes.

Put the tomatoes, garlic, and paprika, if using, into a blender or food processor fitted with a metal blade and pulse until smooth.

Squeeze the water from the bread, add half of it to the tomatoes, and process until fully incorporated. With the machine operating, drop in the remaining bread, a chunk at a time, until all of it has been added.

Season generously with salt and pulse a few times.

With the machine operating, add the vinegar and olive oil. Taste and correct for salt.

Pour the soup, which should be quite thick and creamy, into a bowl, cover, and refrigerate.

To serve, ladle into soup plates.

Working quickly, put the grated egg and parsley into a bowl, season with salt and pepper, toss gently, and sprinkle over the soup. Top with strips of jamón serrano and a drizzle of olive oil and serve immediately.

Smoky Gazpacho

Serves 4 to 6

This version brings a subtle smoky note to the crisp flavors and textures of gazpacho, an effect enhanced by the sherry vinegar. If you have smoked sea salt, which is now widely available, this is an ideal context for it.

1 red onion, peeled and trimmed
2 medium zucchini, trimmed and cut in half lengthwise
3 or 4 small sweet peppers, such as Jimmy Nardello
6 large ripe tomatoes, smoked, peeled, seeded, and minced
6 cloves garlic, minced
¾ teaspoon chipotle powder
Smoked salt or kosher salt
Black pepper in a mill
1 cup chicken stock
3 tablespoons sherry vinegar
2 tablespoons chopped fresh herbs (a mix of Italian parsley, chives, thyme, and oregano)
Best-quality extra-virgin olive oil
1 cup fresh coarse bread crumbs, lightly toasted

Roast the onions, zucchini, and peppers on a grill or under a broiler, turning often, until the skins of the peppers are charred, the onions are browned and partially cooked, and the zucchini is browned and just beginning to soften. Put the peppers in a paper bag until cool, about 20 minutes. Set the onions and zucchini aside to cool.

Remove the peppers' charred skins, stems, and seeds and chop coarsely.

Set a food mill over a deep bowl and grind the tomatoes and peppers through it.

Cut the onion and zucchini into small dice, add to the bowl along with the garlic, and stir.

Season lightly with salt and several turns of pepper.

Stir in the stock, vinegar, and herbs, and cover and chill for at least 2 hours.

To serve, ladle into soup bowls or soup plates, garnish with a drizzle of olive oil, scatter bread crumbs on top, add a pinch of salt to each portion, and serve.

Golden Peach Gazpacho

Serves 3 to 4

In general, I am not a fan of combining tomatoes with other fruits, as I find the pleasing flavors of the ingredients become muddled. Yet when I tasted a nectarine-tomato gazpacho made by my friend Thomas Schmidt, executive chef at John Ash & Co. Restaurant in Santa Rosa, California, I rethought my aversion, as the soup was so delicious. I happened to have my favorite peaches, Arctic Gems from Dry Creek Peach and Produce in Healdsburg, California, on hand, along with some great tomatoes, and so I experimented. I loved the results and am happy to share them with you.

4 medium yellow or orange beefsteak
    tomatoes, peeled, cored, and
    seeded
2 ripe white peaches, peeled
1 serrano, chopped
2 garlic cloves, crushed
Kosher salt

Black pepper in a mill
1 to 2 tablespoons freshly squeezed
    lime juice or sherry vinegar
1 tablespoon best-quality extra-virgin
    olive oil
2 tablespoons chopped fresh cilantro

Put the tomatoes into a blender or a food processor fitted with the metal blade, add the peaches, serrano, and garlic, and pulse several times until smooth. Season with salt, pepper, and lime juice or vinegar and pulse again.

Taste, correct for salt, and pour into a bowl or other container. Cover and refrigerate for at least 3 hours and as long as overnight.

To serve, pour or ladle into soup plates, clear glass mugs, or another attractive dish. Drizzle with a little olive oil, sprinkle with cilantro, add a bit of salt and a turn or two of black pepper, and serve immediately.

Variation:
- Top the soup with a generous spoonful of burrata and several slices of white peach before adding the olive oil and cilantro.

Yogurt and Tomato Soup

Serves 6 to 8

This soup is rich, delicious, healthy, and deeply satisfying. I always have at least a quart of plain yogurt on hand and so it is easy to make on the spur of the moment when tomatoes are in season.

2 cups plain whole milk yogurt
3 to 4 cups fresh Tomato Concassé (page 263)
3 tablespoons extra-virgin olive oil
4 tablespoons lemon juice
4 tablespoons red wine vinegar, medium acid
3 cucumbers, peeled, seeded, and chopped
1 or 2 jalapeños or serranos, stemmed and minced
Kosher salt
Black pepper in a mill
2 tablespoons minced cilantro
2 tablespoons minced mint
2 teaspoons fine lemon zest
½ cup Tomato Essence, page (page 267) optional

Mix together the yogurt, Tomato Concassé, olive oil, lemon juice, and vinegar. Stir in the cucumbers and peppers, taste, and season with salt and pepper. Combine the cilantro, mint, and lemon zest and stir the mixture into the soup. Chill at least 2 hours.

To serve, ladle into wide soup plates and add a swirl of Tomato Essence to each portion.

Tomato Cilantro Soup

Serves 4 to 6

Over the years, I have made and published many versions of this soup, some in columns, others in books, including the first edition of this one. It remains one of my personal favorites and most requested recipes. No book about tomatoes would be complete without this soup, as it is, perhaps, the single best and most versatile tomato soup in the world. It is worth learning by heart so that you no longer need to consult the recipe and can come up with your own variations, based on the time of year, what is fresh in your garden if you have one, and what else is on the menu. When you make it in the winter, be sure to use good canned tomatoes, not those sad fresh ones in supermarkets.

3 tablespoons olive oil
1 medium yellow onion, diced
5 garlic cloves, minced
Kosher salt
Black pepper in a mill
2 cups chicken stock or vegetable stock
3 to 4 pounds ripe red tomatoes, peeled, seeded, and minced
1 tablespoon Madeira
1 bunch cilantro, rinsed, stems discarded
3 tablespoons crème fraîche

Put the olive oil into a medium soup pot set over medium-low heat, add the onion, and sauté until very soft, about 15 to 20 minutes. Do not let it brown. Add the garlic and cook 2 minutes more. Season with salt and pepper.

Add the chicken or vegetable stock and stir in the tomatoes. Increase the heat and when the mixture begins to boil, reduce the heat to low and simmer gently for about 15 minutes.

Remove the soup from the heat and let cool briefly.

Use an immersion blender to purée the soup, add the Madeira, and return to low heat for 5 minutes. Taste and correct the seasoning.

Remove from the heat, stir in the cilantro leaves, and ladle into soup plates.

Stir the crème fraîche to thin it, drizzle some over each portion, and serve immediately.

Variations:

- Serve the soup with a generous dollop of salsa verde.

- Make a sauce of 6 minced garlic cloves, 1 minched serrano, and 1 bunch of minced cilantro leaves combined with ¼ cup fresh lime juice and 3 tablespoons of olive oil. Use chunky or purée with an immersion blender until smooth. Season with salt and swirl over the soup.

- Stir 1 pound of baby Oregon shrimp into the soup and top each portion with minced cucumbers and snipped chives.

- Serve the soup chilled and topped with a generous spoonful of whole milk yogurt.

- Serve the soup chilled and topped with tzatziki, a mixture of whole milk yogurt, minced garlic, minced cucumbers, and salt.

- Omit the cilantro. Stir 2 cups cooked white beans into the soup and mash about half of them against the side of the pan. Stir thoroughly. Add a tablespoon of minced Italian parsley and a tablespoon of minced fresh sage into the soup and serve.

Tomato Broth
with Seed Pasta

Serves 4 to 6

Although this isn't exactly sickbed soup, it is a welcome elixir when you are recovering from an illness. It is light, delicate, and pristine. It is also perfect for a first course at a summer dinner party. There are several varieties of seed pasta, from acini di pepe, which is shaped like peppercorns, Israeli couscous, and orzo to rosamarina and the playful alfabeto, in the shape of tiny letters.

2 tablespoons olive oil
1 small yellow onion, peeled and
    minced
5 garlic cloves, minced
Kosher salt
3 cups tomatoes, peeled, seeded, and
    minced
1 cup Tomato Essence (page 267)

3 cups chicken, smoked chicken, or
    smoked duck stock
4 ounces seed-shaped pasta, cooked
    in salted water until just tender,
    drained
¼ cup Pernod, optional
Black pepper in a mill
¼ cup thinly sliced fresh basil leaves

Heat the olive oil in a heavy soup pot set over medium-low heat and sauté the onion until it is tender and fragrant, about 15 minutes; do not let it brown. Add the garlic and sauté another 2 minutes.

Season with salt.

Stir in the tomatoes, Tomato Essence, and stock and simmer over low heat for 10 minutes. Add the seed pasta and simmer for 2 to 3 minutes, until the pasta is heated through.

Add the Pernod, if using.

Taste the soup, correct for salt, and season with several turns of black pepper. Ladle into warmed soup bowls, top each portion with basil, and serve immediately.

Hearty Summer Tomato Soup

Serves 6 to 8

When you want a more substantial soup that still features the bright taste of summer tomatoes, this is the one. The soup is particularly welcome during a summer storm. You can also use this recipe as a template for winter soups, especially if you have preserved tomatoes from your garden.

½ cup olive oil
2 yellow onions, sliced
3 large shallots, chopped
2 cloves garlic, chopped
Kosher salt
2 carrots, peeled and sliced
2 ribs celery, heavy strings removed, sliced
3 parsley sprigs
l teaspoon sugar
Juice of 1 lemon
1 cup dry white wine
5 cups chicken or duck stock
4 pounds very ripe red tomatoes, peeled, seeded, and chopped
3 tablespoons tomato paste
Black pepper in a mill
½ cup fresh herbs, finely minced (chives, cilantro, Italian parsley, oregano,
    basil, thyme, marjoram)

Heat the olive oil in a large, heavy pot set over medium-low heat, add the onions and shallots, and cook until the vegetables are soft and fragrant, about 15 minutes. Add the garlic and cook 2 minutes.

Season with salt.

Add the carrots, celery, parsley sprigs, sugar, and lemon juice. Stir to blend the mixture, lower the heat, cover, and cook until all the vegetables are tender, about 15 minutes. Pour in the white wine and simmer over medium heat until the wine has nearly completely evaporated. Add 2 cups of the broth, remove from heat, and use tongs to remove and discard the parsley. Purée the mixture with an immersion blender.

Add the chopped tomatoes to the puréed vegetable mixture, stir in the tomato paste, and simmer over low heat for 15 minutes, stirring occasionally so the soup does not burn. Stir in the remaining stock and simmer 30 minutes.

Taste, correct for salt, and season with several turns of black pepper.

Ladle the soup into warm bowls, top each serving with a sprinkling of fresh herbs, and serve immediately.

Tomato & Potato Soup

Serves 4 to 6

When I want a creamy soup, I am much more likely to add potatoes than I am cream, not because I have a problem with cream but because I find it often eclipses other flavors. Potatoes, on the other hand, merge with other ingredients, enhance them, and produce a voluptuous texture.

3 tablespoons olive oil
1 yellow onion, diced
6 cloves garlic, minced
2 jalapeño or serrano, minced
Kosher salt
2 pounds potatoes, such as German Butter, Yukon Gold, or Yellow Finn,
    scrubbed and sliced
3 cups homemade chicken stock
1 28-ounce can peeled whole or sliced tomatoes
Black pepper in a mill
¼ cup chopped fresh Italian parsley

Pour the olive oil into a medium soup pot set over medium-low heat. Add the onion and sauté until it is soft and fragrant, about 15 minutes. Add the garlic and the jalapeño or serrano, sauté 2 minutes more, and add the potatoes. Season with salt and sauté, stirring a time or two, for about 3 minutes.

Pour in the chicken stock along with 3 cups of water, increase the heat, and, when the liquid boils, reduce it so that it simmers gently. Cook for about 15 minutes, until the potatoes are just tender.

Stir in the tomatoes, simmer 10 minutes more, taste, correct for salt, and season with several turns of black pepper.

Stir in the parsley, ladle into soup bowls, and serve.

For a creamy soup, purée with an immersion blender before serving.

Variations:

- Serve the puréed soup with a dollop of cilantro sauce (see below).

- Use a small yellow onion and the white and pale green parts of 2 leeks and continue as directed in the main recipe. Omit the jalapeño or serrano, add the zest of 1 lemon when you add the tomatoes, and serve with lime wedges alongside.

Cilantro Sauce

To make cilantro sauce, place 6 cloves of peeled garlic, 1 de-stemmed serrano pepper, and 1 bunch of cilantro, stems discarded, in a blender or food processor. Add ¼ cup fresh lime juice, 3 tablespoons extra-virgin olive oil, and 1 teaspoon kosher salt. Process until smooth. This sauce will keep in a refrigerator for 3 to 4 days.

Tomato Bread Soup

Serves 4

Bread soups are versatile, delicious, and very easy to make, especially when you keep a supply of homemade stocks in the freezer. It is also helpful to save stale bread. The best way to do this is, when you find you have leftover hearth bread, cut it into 1-inch cubes, pack it into heavy plastic bags, and store it in the freezer. With these two items on hand, you'll have a fabulous soup on the table in less than 20 minutes.

3 tablespoons olive oil
1 yellow onion, chopped
6 or 7 garlic cloves, crushed and minced
Kosher salt
4 cups ripe red tomatoes (about 2 pounds), peeled, seeded, and chopped, or
    1 32-ounce can of diced or crushed tomatoes
4 cups homemade chicken stock
Black pepper in a mill and kosher salt
About 3 cups good, crusty day-old bread, torn or cut into 1-inch pieces
Extra-virgin olive oil
4 tablespoons chopped Italian parsley
Parmigiano-Reggiano or similar cheese, in one piece, optional

Pour the olive oil into a medium soup pot, add the onion, and sauté until soft and fragrant. Add the garlic and sauté 2 minutes more. Season with salt.

Add the tomatoes and simmer for 3 minutes. Add the stock and several turns of black pepper and simmer 5 minutes more.

Add the bread, stir, cover, and set aside for 5 to 10 minutes.

Taste and correct for salt.

Ladle into soup bowls, top with a drizzle of olive oil, some Italian parsley, and a bit of grated cheese, if using. Serve immediately.

Summer Shell Bean
and Tomato Soup

Serves 4 to 6

More and more farmers are growing shell beans and offering them at farmers markets in late summer and early fall. When they are available fresh—it's a short season—try this soup, as there is nothing as delicious as fresh heirloom shell beans. At other times of year, make this soup with a dried white shell bean, such as cannellini or marrowfats. To make this soup with dried beans, consult the variation at the end of the main recipe.

10 to 12 ounces fresh white shell beans, cooked, or 8 ounces dried white
    shell beans, cooked (see Note on next page)
2 tablespoons olive oil
3 ounces pancetta, diced
2 large shallots, minced
4 cloves garlic, crushed and minced
Kosher salt
3 cups Tomato Concassé (page 263)
3 cups homemade chicken or duck stock
Black pepper in a mill
¼ cup minced fresh herbs (thyme, marjoram, oregano, summer savory, Italian
    parsley)

Cook the beans if you have not already done so.

Pour the olive oil into a medium soup pot set over medium-low heat, add the pancetta, and cook until it loses its raw look, about 8 to 10 minutes. Add the shallots and cook until soft and fragrant, about 8 minutes more. Add the garlic, cook for 2 minutes more, and season lightly with salt.

Add the Tomato Concassé, the stock, and the cooked beans, cover, and simmer gently for 15 minutes.

Taste, correct for salt, and season with several turns of black pepper. Ladle into soup bowls, sprinkle with herbs, and serve immediately.

> **Variation:**
> - For a creamy soup, use an immersion blender to purée all or a portion of the soup, until it reaches the texture you seek, after it is fully cooked.

NOTE

Cook fresh shell beans in plenty of lightly salted water until they are just tender. The time will vary based on the type of bean but nearly all varieties are done within 20 to 25 minutes. To cook dried shell beans, soak the beans in plenty of water for several hours or overnight. Drain the beans, put them into a large pot, cover with water by at least 2 inches, add a bay leaf, bring to a boil, reduce the heat, and simmer gently until the beans are tender, about 35 to 60 minutes, depending on the bean itself and its age. When the beans are not quite tender but have begun to release their aromas, season the beans with salt. Stir now and then during cooking and add water as needed to keep the beans from scorching. Remove from the heat, let rest, and drain.

A Tomato Cookbook

Tomato & Corn Chowder
with Salmon, Ginger & Lemongrass

Serves 6

This soup is inspired by the wild Pacific King salmon that is in season where I live in Northern California at the same time local tomatoes are at their best. If you don't have access to this salmon, I recommend using whatever wild salmon may be available to you. I do not recommend using farmed salmon. You can also make a delicious version with dry-smoked salmon (from wild salmon, please).

3 tablespoons olive oil
1 yellow onion, peeled and diced
3 cloves garlic, minced
l serrano pepper, stem removed, minced
Kosher salt
2-inch piece of ginger, peeled, chopped, and squeezed through a garlic press
l quart fish stock, hot (see Note on next page)
2 stalks lemongrass, bruised and cut into l-inch pieces
Juice of l lime
½ cup dry white wine
2 medium tomatoes, peeled, seeded, and diced
1 cup fresh corn kernels
1 pound wild Pacific King salmon fillet, skinned and cut into 1½-inch cubes
¾ cup coconut milk
¼ cup cilantro leaves
Kosher salt and freshly milled black pepper

Pour the olive oil into a medium soup pot set over medium-low heat, add the onion, and sauté the onion until soft and fragrant, about 15 minutes. Add the garlic and serrano, sauté 2 minutes more, and season with salt.

Add the ginger, fish stock, and lemongrass, lower the heat, cover, and simmer 15 minutes. Add the lime juice, wine, and tomatoes and simmer another 15 minutes.

Use tongs to remove and discard the lemongrass. Add the corn and the salmon and let the soup simmer *very* gently for a scant 2 minutes. Stir in the coconut milk and cilantro and heat through.

Taste, correct for salt, and season with several generous turns of black pepper.

Ladle into soup plates and serve hot.

NOTE

To make fish stock, put 3 pounds of fish heads and fish frames, 1 large quartered yellow onion, 2 or 3 sprigs Italian parsley, 1 bay leaf, ½ lemon, 1 cup dry white wine, 1 teaspoon black peppercorns, and 4 cups water in a large soup kettle. Bring the mixture to a boil, reduce the heat, skim off any foam that forms, and simmer for 30 minutes. Strain, cool, and refrigerate it for up to 3 days. You may also freeze fish stock. As a substitute for true stock, you can use a mixture of 2 parts clam juice, 1 part white wine, 1 part water, and the juice of 1 lemon.

A Tomato Cookbook

Thai-Style Chicken Soup
with Tomatoes, Coconut Milk & Cilantro

Serves 6 to 8

Meat of any kind is always best when it is cooking on the bone. In Southeast Asia, it is quite common to find both chicken and duck in soups. If you are used to boneless, skinless chicken breast it may take some time to enjoy it this way but it will have so much more flavor and such a better texture that you will come to prefer it. Simply add little plates next to each bowl for discarding the bones. To cut the chicken into pieces, you'll need both a sharp cleaver and a heavy, sturdy wood cutting board. If you don't have these items, you might be able to talk your local butcher into cutting the chicken for you.

3 chicken leg-thigh pieces, bone in, preferably from pastured chickens
2 tablespoons peanut oil
2 shallots, minced
½ cup scallions, very thinly sliced
3 cloves garlic, minced
2 serranos, minced
1 tablespoon fresh ginger, grated
Kosher salt
3 cups homemade chicken stock
3 stalks lemongrass, bruised and cut into 1-inch pieces

Juice of 2 limes
3 tablespoons fish sauce (Nam Pla)
2 cups fresh Tomato Concassé
3 cups coconut milk
Palm sugar or granulated sugar, optional
Kosher salt
¼ cup minced fresh cilantro leaves
Lime wedges

Set the chicken, one piece at a time, on a heavy, clean work surface and use a large meat cleaver to hack each thigh and leg into 3 or 4 crosswise pieces about 1½ inches long, hacking through the bone.

Pour the oil into a large soup pot set over medium-low heat, add the shallots, and sauté until soft and fragrant. Add the scallions and sauté until limp, add the garlic, serranos, and ginger, and sauté another 2 minutes.

Add the chicken and cook for about 3 minutes, turning once, to brown the chicken lightly. Season with a little salt.

Stir in the stock, lemongrass, lime juice, fish sauce, and Tomato Concassé. Bring the soup to a simmer, reduce the heat to very low, cover the pot, and simmer about 15 minutes, until the chicken is just cooked through. Do not overcook.

Stir in the coconut milk, heat through, and taste. If it tastes a bit flat or if the flavor of the coconut hasn't quite blossomed, add sugar, a teaspoon at a time, until the flavors emerge. Correct for acid with a bit more lime juice and for salt with a bit more fish sauce.

Ladle into soup bowls, scatter cilantro leaves on top, and serve immediately, with lime wedges alongside.

Pasta Fagioli Soup

Serves 4

There are endless variations of this traditional Italian soup, and I've never had one I didn't enjoy. I particularly like this one in fall, when the weather is turning cool but a few of summer's tomatoes linger. If you do not have duck stock, use rich homemade chicken, veal, or beef stock. Commercial broth will not provide the richness of both taste and texture the soup requires. The soup is delicious topped with Pistou (page 253), Red Chimichurri (page 251), and Red Chermoula (page 252).

2 tablespoons olive oil
1 yellow onion, diced
6 to 8 cloves garlic, minced
Kosher salt
Generous pinch of crushed red
    pepper flakes
1 cup Tomato Concassé (page 263)
    or Tomato Essence (page 267)
2 cups concentrated duck stock
    (4 cups normal strength reduced
    to 2 cups)

2 cups cooked cannellini beans
2 medium fresh tomatoes, in season
4 ounces (1 cup) small dry pasta, such
    as ditalini or tripolini
3 tablespoons chopped fresh Italian
    parsley
Black pepper in a mill
Fresh Parmigiano-Reggiano or
    similar hard cheese, in one piece,
    or Pecorino Romano cheese

Heat the olive oil in a medium soup pot set over medium-low heat, add the onion, and sauté until limp and transparent, about 15 minutes. Add the garlic and sauté 2 minutes more. Season with salt and add the crushed red pepper flakes.

Stir in the Tomato Concassé or Tomato Essence, the duck stock, and 2 cups of water. Bring to a boil, add the beans and tomatoes, lower the heat, and simmer for 20 minutes. Stir in the pasta and cook until it is just tender. Remove from the heat, cover, and let rest for about 10 minutes. Stir in the Italian parsley and several turns of black pepper, taste, and correct for salt.

Remove the soup from the heat. Ladle the soup into bowls, grate cheese on top, and serve immediately.

White Bean, Tomato & Chorizo Soup
with Cilantro

Serves 6 to 8

Use the best chorizo you can find but avoid the Mexican chorizos that are packed in plastic casings, as they contain way too much fat and will ruin rather than enhance the soup. Andouille, linguiça, and kielbasa are good substitutes when you can't find chorizo.

8 ounces dry cannellini or other white beans
Kosher salt
3 tablespoons olive oil
1 yellow onion, chopped
6 cloves garlic, crushed and minced
1 jalapeño or serrano pepper,
    minced
1 28-ounce can diced tomatoes or crushed tomatoes
1 pound Spanish-style fresh chorizo, cooked until just done
Black pepper in a mill
1 poblano, roasted, peeled, seeded, and cut into small julienne
½ cup cilantro leaves

Soak the beans overnight in enough water to cover them plus 4 to 5 inches.

Drain and rinse the beans.

Put the beans into a large, heavy pot, cover with fresh water by at least 2 inches, set over high heat, and, when the water boils, reduce the heat so that the beans simmer gently. When they are about two-thirds done—you'll notice they are beginning to smell like beans—season them with salt. Stir now and then and add water if needed to keep the beans from drying out.

Meanwhile, pour the olive oil into a heavy sauté pan set over medium-low heat, add the onion, and sauté until soft and fragrant, about 15 minutes. Add the garlic and jalapeño or serrano, sauté 2 minutes more, and season with salt.

When the beans are tender, stir in the onion mixture along with the tomatoes.

Working quickly, cut the chorizo into ¼-inch-thick rounds and then cut the rounds in half, making half moons. Stir into the soup, cover, and simmer very gently for 25 to 30 minutes.

Remove from the heat and let rest for10 to 15 minutes.

Taste, correct for salt, and season with several generous turns of black pepper.

Ladle into soup bowls, top each portion with julienned poblano and cilantro, and serve immediately.

Italian-Style Fish Soup
with Crab

Serves 3 to 4

In California, fresh crab is a winter specialty and so we must use preserved or canned tomatoes should we want to combine the two. This soup, inspired by one from the southern coast of Italy, is both delicious and very easy to make either with whatever local crab you have available or other fish and shellfish.

1½ cup shellfish stock (see Note on next page)
½ cup extra-virgin olive oil, plus more for drizzling
1 shallot, minced
3 garlic cloves, very thinly sliced
Kosher salt
Black pepper in a mill
1 teaspoon red pepper flakes
2 tablespoons double-concentrated tomato paste
½ cup dry white white
Meat from 1 freshly cooked Dungeness crab
1 tablespoon minced fresh oregano
Italian parsley leaves, for garnish
Sourdough hearth bread, hot

First, make the shellfish stock if you do not have it on hand (it is a good thing to keep in the freezer).

Heat the ½ cup olive oil in a heavy saucepan set over medium heat. Add the shallots, fry 3 to 4 minutes, add the garlic, and fry 1 minute more. Do not let the garlic or shallots burn. Season generously with salt and pepper.

Reduce the heat to low and stir in the pepper flakes, tomato paste, and wine. Add the shellfish stock and simmer until the liquid just begins to thicken, about 5 minutes.

Add the crab and the oregano, cover the pan, and remove from the heat. Let sit for 5 minutes so the crab heats through.

Ladle into warm soup plates, garnish with Italian parsley leaves, and drizzle each portion with olive oil. Serve immediately, with hot bread alongside.

NOTE

To make shellfish stock you will first need to make fish fumet. To do so, rinse 2½ to 3 pounds fish heads, tails, and bones in cold water to remove bits of blood and innards. Drain and put the fish in a stockpot. Add a quartered onion, 2 small stalks of celery, a teaspoon of peppercorns, a bay leaf, 4 sprigs of Italian parsley, 3 sprigs of thyme, a cup of dry white wine, and 8 cups of water. Bring to a boil over medium-high heat. Reduce the heat to low, skim off any foam that forms, and simmer 30 minutes. Strain and cool the liquid.

While the fumet cooks, sauté the shells of a Dungeness crab—rinsed and chopped—in 2 tablespoons of olive oil, stirring constantly. Add 2 cups water and simmer until the water is nearly completely evaporated. Add the fish fumet and simmer 10 minutes. Strain the stock into a clean container. Use immediately or store in the refrigerator for 2 days or the freezer for up to 3 months.

Tomato & Crab Bisque
with Ginger & Golden Caviar

Serves 4 to 6

On the West Coast, we are blessed with plump Dungeness crab from November through spring, though the season typically peaks around the winter holidays. This bisque, which admittedly takes a bit of time to make, is a delicious way to celebrate the Dungeness crab, which aficionados, myself among them, believe is the most delicious shellfish in the world. Except for oysters. Oh, and clams. And razor clams. Well, what can I say other than that it is really, really good? To serve as a main course, simply double the amount of crab.

3 tablespoons butter
1 yellow onion, diced
Kosher salt
1 quart homemade chicken stock
3-inch piece of fresh ginger, thinly sliced
1 large or 2 small–medium Dungeness crabs, cooked and cleaned
1 cup dry white wine

¼ cup crème fraîche
3 ounces golden caviar
3 tablespoons minced fresh chives
1 lemon wedge
1 28-ounce can diced or crushed tomatoes
Black pepper in a mill
3 or 4 tablespoons Rainwater Madeira or medium-dry sherry

Melt 2 tablespoons of the butter in a soup pot set over medium-low heat. Add the onion and sauté until the onion is soft and transparent and just beginning to caramelize, about 25 minutes; do not let it brown. Season with a little salt, add the chicken stock and half the ginger, and simmer over low heat for 30 minutes. While the stock is simmering, pick the crabmeat and reserve the shells. Put the body meat into a medium bowl, set whole legs on top, cover, and refrigerate.

Set a medium sauté pan over medium heat, melt the remaining tablespoon of butter, add the crab shells, and sauté, turning frequently, for about 5 minutes. Increase the heat to high, add the wine, and boil until it is reduced by about two-thirds. Tip the shells and pan juices into the simmering stock, cover, and simmer 30 minutes more.

A Tomato Cookbook

Meanwhile, put the crème fraîche into a small bowl, add the caviar and 1 tablespoon of the chives, and stir. Squeeze a little lemon juice into the mixture and stir again. Cover and refrigerate.

Set a strainer over a clean pot and pour the stock through the strainer. Discard the aromatics and crab shells.

With the strained stock over medium-low heat, stir in the tomatoes and remaining slices of ginger and simmer for 15 minutes.

(The soup can be made in advance up to this point. Let it rest until you are ready to finish it.)

To finish, strain the soup a final time, return it to the heat, and simmer until reduced by one-quarter to one-third. Taste, correct for salt, and season with several turns of black pepper. Add the Madeira or sherry and heat through.

Set individual soup plates on a work surface and divide the body meat of the crab among them. Ladle the soup over the crab and set crab legs on top. Add a large dollop of caviar cream, scatter with chives, and serve immediately.

Tomato Stilton Soup
with Fried Sage Leaves

Serves 6 to 8

If you want a spectacular starter for Thanksgiving dinner, begin your meal with this rich soup fragrant with sage and full of delightful layers of flavor. When I first developed this soup, there was no local blue cheese. Now that we have wonderful artisan producers, I often use, say, Point Reyes Bay Blue from Point Reyes Farmstead Cheese Company.

3 tablespoons olive oil
2 medium leeks (about 1 cup), white and pale green parts, washed, drained, and thinly sliced
1 white or yellow onion, diced
2 tablespoons minced garlic
Kosher salt
1 28-ounce can crushed peeled tomatoes, or 4 cups peeled, seeded, and minced beefsteak tomatoes
4 cups homemade chicken stock
2 tablespoons finely minced fresh sage leaves
24 medium fried sage leaves (see Note on next page)
4 to 6 ounces (1 to 1½ cups) crumbled Stilton or other blue-veined cheese, to taste
Black pepper in a mill

Pour the olive oil into a heavy soup pot set over medium-low heat, add the leeks and onions, and sauté until they are soft and fragrant, about 15 minutes. Add the garlic and cook for an additional 2 minutes. Season lightly with salt.

Stir in the tomatoes, stock, and sage and bring the mixture to a boil. Reduce the heat and simmer gently for 15 minutes.

While the soup cooks, prepare the fried sage leaves.

Add the cheese and stir constantly over low heat until it is just melted; do not let the soup boil. Add several generous turns of pepper, ladle into soup plates, top with fried sage leaves, and serve immediately.

NOTE

To fry sage leaves, select large blemish-free sage leaves, rinse them under cool water, and set on a tea towel. Pat the leaves dry. Pour a thin layer of olive oil into a small, heavy saucepan and set over medium heat for about 2 minutes. Carefully add a single leaf and if it sizzles, add 3 to 4 more. If it doesn't sizzle, wait until it does, turn over, and cook 5 seconds more. If the leaf curls, use a dinner fork to hold it flat. Transfer the cooked leaf or leaves to a paper towel folded into fourths and continue cooking —about 5 to 6 seconds per side—until all the leaves have been fried. Sprinkle very lightly with salt and use within 30 minutes or so.

Posole Rojo

Makes 8 to 10 servings

Posole became a Halloween tradition among my closest friends many years ago, when I agreed to bring it to the home of my friends Una Glass and Michael Kyes, which was centrally located and perfect as a home base while kids of all ages trick-or-treated. That year, I made two versions, Posole Rojo, with tomatoes, and Posole Verde, with poblanos and other chilies but no tomatoes. The next year I asked Una and Michael what they were doing on Halloween and Michael replied, "Eating your posole?"

A tradition was born. Little did we know at the time that in a decade or so, I would be preparing both versions in mid-July 2014 for Michael's memorial service. We all agreed that it would be the perfect thing to serve as we celebrated his life.

4 pounds pork shoulder or butt
2 tablespoons kosher salt, plus more as needed
2 teaspoons chipotle powder
3 tablespoons olive oil
1 large yellow onion, diced
2 serranos, stems removed, minced
6 garlic cloves
2 teaspoons dried oregano, preferably Mexican
Black pepper, freshly ground .
2 to 3 dried chilies, preferably ancho or pasilla, soaked in hot water, drained, peeled, and seeded

6 cups homemade chicken stock or broth
2 28-ounce cans diced tomatoes, preferably Muir Glen brand
2 28-ounce cans hominy
2 limes, cut into wedges
½ cup minced fresh cilantro leaves
½ cup minced white onion
½ white cabbage, thinly shredded
2 dozen small corn tortillas, hot
Bottle Mexican hot sauce, such as Cholula or Tapatio

Set the pork on a clean work surface.

In a small bowl, mix together the 2 tablespoons kosher salt and the chipotle powder, if using, and rub the mixture into the pork. Set the pork in a clay cooker or other ovenproof container, add 1 cup water, cover, and set on the middle rack of the oven. Turn the heat to 250°F and cook until the meat is very tender, 4 to 5 hours.

Meanwhile, heat the olive oil in a large soup pot set over medium heat, add the onion, and sauté until limp and fragrant, about 15 minutes, stirring frequently. Do not let the onion brown. Add the serranos and garlic, sauté 2 minutes more, and stir in the oregano. Season with salt and several turns of black pepper.

Put the dried chili into a suribachi or molcajete and grind it into a paste. Add the chili paste, chicken stock, tomatoes, and hominy to the onion mixture. Increase the heat to high, bring to a boil, reduce the heat to low, and simmer, partially covered, for 45 minutes.

When the pork is tender, transfer it to a work surface and pour the pan liquid into a transparent container. Skim off and discard the fat and pour the juices into the soup.

Use a large knife or cleaver to hack the meat into small pieces and stir them into the soup.

Simmer the soup 30 minutes more. Taste and correct the seasoning.

To serve, ladle the soup into bowls. Arrange the limes, cilantro, onion, and cabbage in a wide, shallow bowl and wrap the hot tortillas in a warm tea towel.

Serve the soup immediately, with the condiments and tortillas alongside.

A Tomato Cookbook

Seafood Posole

Serves 6 to 8

Many seafood soups and stews taste overly fishy, a result of cooking the seafood too long and using poorly made fish fumet. In this recipe, adapted from a seafood stew I've been making for a couple of decades, I use chicken stock instead of fish fumet and add the seafood at the last minute, so it retains its bright flavors and tender texture. The stew calls for achiote, a paste of spices and annatto seed that you can find in Latino markets; if you do not have it, you can make a delicious stew without it.

Cilantro Sauce, page 95
3 tablespoons olive oil
1 yellow onion, diced
2 to 3 serranos, minced
8 garlic cloves, minced
2 teaspoons achiote paste (available at Latino markets)
1 or 2 dried chilies, preferably ancho or pasilla, soaked in hot water, drained, peeled, and seeded
6 cups chicken stock
Kosher salt
Black pepper in a mill
1 28-ounce can hominy (pozole), drained
3 medium zucchini, cut into small dice
2 pounds ripe tomatoes, peeled, seeded, minced, and drained
1 pound fish fillets, such as snapper, butterfish, or other rockfish, in 1-inch cubes
2 pounds cockles, Manila clams, or black mussels, thoroughly washed
1 lime, in wedges
2 cups shredded cabbage
Hot corn tortillas

Heat the olive oil in a large soup pot set over low heat. Add the onion and serranos and sauté until soft and fragrant, about 15 minutes. Add the garlic and sauté 2 minutes more.

Break up the achiote and put it in a small bowl. Add enough of the chicken stock to make a paste; put the paste, the dried chilies, and the remaining chicken stock into the pot with the onion mixture. Season with salt, add the hominy, and simmer for 10 minutes. And the zucchini and tomatoes and simmer 10 minutes more.

Add the seafood to the soup, stir gently, and simmer 5 minutes. Remove the pot from the heat, cover, and let rest 5 minutes. Discard any shellfish that have not opened.

To serve, ladle into soup plates, top with a generous dollop of Cilantro Sauce, and serve immediately, with lime wedges, shredded cabbage, hot tortillas, and the remaining sauce alongside.

Creamy Tomato Soup
in Puff Pastry

Serves 6 to 8

Bistro Jeanty in Yountville, California, may be best known for its Cream of Tomato Soup in Puff Pastry, which is served year-round. The restaurant also shares its recipe on its website, though I came by it when I was writing an article about winter soups for Savor Wine Country Magazine. This version is inspired by theirs, though it is not identical. If you enjoy making your own puff pastry, by all means do so. But don't feel like you must; commercial puff pastry is just fine in this context.

½ cup unsalted butter
2 large yellow onions, very thinly sliced
6 garlic cloves, crushed and minced
Kosher salt
1 bay leaf
1 tablespoon whole black peppercorns
1 teaspoon dried thyme leaves
¼ cup tomato paste

1 32-ounce can crushed or diced tomatoes
1 cup chicken stock
3 cups heavy cream
3 tablespoons salted butter
White pepper in a mill
1 pound puff pastry, cold
1 egg, well beaten with 1 tablespoon of water

Melt the butter in a large soup pot set over medium-low heat, add the onions, and cook gently until very soft and fragrant, about 15 minutes. Add the garlic and sauté 1 minute more.

Season with salt.

Add the bay leaf, peppercorns, thyme, and tomato paste, then cover and cook, stirring all the while, for 5 minutes to lightly toast the paste.

Stir in the tomatoes and chicken stock and simmer over low heat for 30 to 40 minutes, until both the tomatoes and onions have fallen apart. Remove from the heat and let cool slightly.

Set a food mill over a deep bowl or pot and pass the tomato mixture through it. If you do not have a food mill, purée with an immersion blender and strain to remove the bay leaf and peppercorns.

Return the soup to a clean pot set over medium-low heat.

Stir in the cream and heat through. Taste, correct for salt, and season with several turns of white pepper.

To finish the soup, preheat the oven to 450°F and set ovenproof bowls or ramekins on your work surface.

Cut rounds of puff pastry about 1 inch bigger than the opening of the containers and brush their surfaces with the egg wash.

Ladle soup into the containers, leaving about ¾ of an inch at the top. Carefully top each container with a round of dough, washed side down, pulling gently to stretch it over the container and pressing it to the side, as if you were making a tight drum.

Carefully set the containers on a baking sheet, set in the oven, and cook for 12 to 15 minutes, until the dough is puffed and golden brown. Do not open the oven for at least 10 minutes.

Carefully transfer to plates and serve immediately.

Salads

Summer Tomato Salads

A salad of fresh tomatoes made from the best-tasting tomatoes you can find is one of the purest pleasures of summer. At the height of the season, I enjoy such a salad once a day or more, varying the additions with what is on hand and what tempts me at a particular time. The entire process, from the picking (or buying or begging) of the tomato, to its slicing and arranging on a plate, takes little time and is an entirely pleasing activity. It is essential that you use not only the best tomatoes you can find, but those appropriate to the style of preparation. For example, plum tomatoes, with their dense flesh, are not well suited to salads, nor are tomatoes with large, juicy seed pockets, unless they happen to taste particularly wonderful.

I have never been a fan of tossing a handful of tomato wedges into a green salad, especially when tomatoes are not in season. I prefer to enjoy the greens for themselves, accented occasionally by sliced red onion or thinly sliced radishes.

Out-of-Season Tomato Salads

Just don't and if you do, stop.

If you must, use dried-tomato bits in Winter Bread Salad (page 141).

If for some reason you must break this cardinal tomato rule, here is some advice. If you can, use cherry tomatoes, cut them in half, sprinkle with salt, and let rest at least fifteen minutes before using. If you must use sliced tomatoes, cut them through their equators, set in a single layer on a plate, sprinkle with salt, and let rest thirty minutes. The salt will draw out as much flavor as possible from these sad creatures.

Sliced Tomato Salad with Eleven Variations
with Italian Parsley and Garlic
with Italian Parsley, Garlic & Grated Cheese
with Shaved Parmigiano-Reggiano and Garlic
with Mozzarella Fresca and Fresh Basil
with Peppers and Cucumbers
with Sliced Lemons
with Lime, Chilies & Cilantro
with Preserved Lemons and Green Olives
with Tuna and Lemon
with Anchovies, Onions & Olives
with Feta Cheese, Oregano, Olives & Anchovies

Cherry Tomato Salad with Three Variations
with Preserved Lemons
Mexican-Style
Greek-Style

Cherry Tomatoes with Grilled Sweet Onions, Bacon,
and Honey-Pepper Vinaigrette
Tomato Avocado Salad
Insalata Caprese with Burrata
Traditional Insalata Caprese
Tomatoes with Sweet Onions and Sardines
Farm Market Salad
Lakeville Tabbouleh
Bread Salad with Cherry Tomatoes, Sausage & Chimichurri
Greek-Inspired Bread Salad
Winter Bread Salad
Red Wine Vinaigrette

A Tomato Cookbook

Sliced Tomato Salad
with Eleven Variations

Serves 4

Recipes for sliced tomato salads are not really necessary if you understand a few simple rules. First, choose one large or two medium tomatoes per person, or more if the salad will be the main part of the meal. Don't worry about peeling the tomatoes, as these salads are casual, not refined. Salads starring unpeeled tomatoes offer up summer's simplest, rustic pleasures.

Next, you must slice the tomato through its equator, not through its poles—that is, horizontally, not vertically. You are making slices, not wedges. If you look at a tomato as a tiny globe, its blossom end is the south pole, the stem end the north pole. Its fat middle is the center, its equator. Cut the tomato in ¼-inch slices parallel with the equator. Discard the pole ends and arrange the thick slices on a plate or platter.

Drizzle your sliced tomatoes with a little extra-virgin olive oil—this is a time to use the very best you have, as its flavors and textures will be center stage—and add a sprinkling of flake salt and freshly ground black pepper. Be sure to have plenty of good, crusty bread on hand to soak up the delicious juices. And, finally, if you have access to a variety of heirloom tomatoes, use several for a visually striking and delicious salad.

4 large tomatoes, sliced
Flake salt
Black pepper in a mill
Extra-virgin olive oil

Arrange the sliced tomatoes on one large or four individual plates. Drizzle with olive oil, and season with salt and pepper. Let the salad rest for 10 or 15 minutes so that the flavors can mingle, but be sure to serve within the hour.

Variations:

- Italian Parsley and Garlic: Sprinkle 2 or 3 cloves of crushed and minced garlic and 3 tablespoons minced fresh Italian parsley over the tomatoes before adding the olive oil.

- Italian Parsley, Garlic, and Grated Cheese: Sprinkle 2 or 3 cloves of crushed and minced garlic and 3 tablespoons minced fresh Italian parsley over the tomatoes before adding the olive oil. Scatter 2 ounces of grated hard cheese (Dry Jack, Parmigiano-Reggiano, or similar cheese) over the tomatoes after the olive oil has been added.

- Shaved Parmigiano-Reggiano and Garlic: Sprinkle 2 cloves of crushed and minced garlic over the tomatoes before adding the olive oil. Using a vegetable peeler, make 15 to 20 curls of Parmigiano-Reggiano and scatter them over the tomatoes.

- Mozzarella Fresca and Fresh Basil: Tuck 8 slices (about 4 ounces) of mozzarella fresca here and there between the slices of tomato before adding the olive oil. Cut 10 to 12 leaves of fresh basil into very thin, lengthwise strips and scatter them over the surface of the salad.

- Peppers and Cucumbers: Before adding the olive oil, scatter 2 or 3 cloves of crushed and minced garlic over the tomatoes. Cut 2 medium lemon cucumbers or 1 large lemon cucumber into very thin slices and tuck them in between slices of tomatoes. Cut 1 jalapeño or serrano into thin rounds and tuck them here and there between the tomatoes and cucumbers.

- Sliced Lemons: Slice 1 lemon into very thin rounds and tuck the slices here and there between the slices of tomato before adding the olive oil.

- Lime, Chilies, and Cilantro: Cut 1 lime into very thin slices and tuck here and there between the tomatoes. Remove the stems and seeds and cut 1 jalapeño or serrano into thin julienne and scatter the peppers over the surface of the salad before adding the olive oil. Add the olive oil, salt, and pepper, and then sprinkle ¼ cup fresh cilantro leaves over everything.

- Preserved Lemons and Green Olives: Scatter ¼ cup thinly sliced preserved lemons, and ¼ cup pitted and sliced green olives such as

A Tomato Cookbook

picholines over the tomatoes before adding olive oil. Add the olive oil, salt, and pepper, and then sprinkle with 1 tablespoon minced fresh oregano leaves.

- Tuna and Lemon: Drain a 6½-ounce can of imported tuna and scatter the tuna over the tomatoes before adding the olive oil. Add 2 or 3 cloves of crushed and minced garlic. Drizzle with the olive oil and squeeze the juice of ½ lemon over the salad before adding salt and pepper.

- Anchovies, Onions, and Olives: Peel a small sweet red onion and slice it into very thin rounds. Add the onion slices randomly on top of the tomatoes and then drape 6 to 8 anchovy fillets, cut in half, over the onions and tomatoes. Scatter ¾ cup pitted Kalamata or Niçoise olives over the salad, and then add the olive oil, salt, and pepper.

- Feta Cheese, Oregano, Olives, and Anchovies: Soak 8 anchovy fillets in 2 tablespoons red wine vinegar for 30 minutes. Drain the anchovies, cut each fillet in half, and scatter over the tomatoes. Cut 2 ounces feta cheese into small cubes and scatter them on top, followed by ¼ cup pitted and chopped Kalamata olives. Drizzle with olive oil, season with salt and pepper, and scatter 1 tablespoon minced fresh oregano leaves on top.

Cherry Tomato Salad
with Three Variations

Serves 4 to 6

Cherry tomato plants are notoriously productive and it can be hard to keep up with them at the height of their season. This casual salad is a great way to enjoy them day after day.

1 quart cherry tomatoes, a mix of colors, halved
6 cloves garlic, minced
2 ounces grated cheese, such as Dry Jack, Asiago, or similar cheese (Dry Jack, Parmesan, Asiago, Romano)
Kosher salt
⅓ cup best-quality extra-virgin olive oil
Black pepper in a mill
2 tablespoons snipped fresh chives, or 2 tablespoons thinly sliced basil

Put the tomatoes into a medium serving bowl, add the garlic and cheese, and season lightly with salt. Add the olive oil and several generous turns of black pepper. Sprinkle with chives or basil, let rest 10 or 15 minutes, and serve.

Variations:

- Preserved Lemons: Add ¼ cup chopped preserved lemons to the salad and omit the salt.

- Mexican-Style: Omit the chives. Add 1 minced serrano, ¼ cup chopped cilantro leaves, and 1 tablespoon fresh lime juice.

- Greek-Style: Replace the grated cheese with crumbled feta. Add 2 tablespoons minced red onion, 2 tablespoons red wine vinegar, and 1 tablespoon minced fresh oregano; omit the chives.

Cherry Tomatoes
with Grilled Sweet Onions, Bacon
& Honey-Pepper Vinaigrette

Serves 6 to 8

This salad can be made with any onion but it is best with a sweet one, such as Vidalia, Walla Walla, or Maui. This is a great side dish for a summer barbecue. It travels well, too, making it perfect for a potluck or picnic.

4 medium or 2 large sweet onions, peeled and cut in half through their equators
Olive oil
1 shallot, minced
3 cloves garlic, minced
Kosher salt
2 tablespoons sherry vinegar
2 tablespoons balsamic vinegar
¼ cup honey, warmed
2 tablespoons freshly ground black pepper
⅔ cup extra-virgin olive oil
¼ pound thick-sliced bacon, fried until crisp, drained
1 quart cherry tomatoes, mixed colors, quartered
1 tablespoon minced fresh Italian parsley
1 tablespoon snipped fresh chives

Prepare a fire in a charcoal grill.

When the coals are ready, brush the onions with olive oil and grill, turning often, until they are tender all the way through. Transfer to a work surface and let rest.

Meanwhile, make the vinaigrette. Put the shallot and garlic into a small bowl, add a generous pinch of salt, and pour in the sherry vinegar. Set aside for 15 minutes. Add the balsamic vinegar, honey, and black pepper. Taste and correct for salt, making it a tad saltier than you prefer.

Chop or crumble the bacon.

Put the cherry tomatoes into a large bowl.

Cut the grilled onions into small dice and add them to the bowl.

Quickly whisk the vinaigrette and pour half of it over the salad. Toss gently and correct for salt and peper.

Cut the cherry tomatoes in half or in quarters, depending on size, and place them in a large bowl. Discard the outer skins and cores of the onions, chop them coarsely, and add them to the bowl with the tomatoes. Add the vinaigrette, toss gently, and taste. Correct for salt, add the parsley and chives, and toss again.

Divide the salad among individual plates or mound onto a serving platter. Scatter the bacon on top and serve.

To transport the salad for a picnic or potluck, do not add the bacon. Pack the salad into a leakproof container and set it into a thermal bag. Wrap the bacon in a piece of aluminum foil and scatter on the salad immediately before serving it.

Variations:
- Pasta Salad: Cook 8 ounces (dry) small shells, tripolini, or farfallini in salted water until just done. Rinse in cool water and drain thoroughly. Grill 1 small onion and continue as directed in the main recipe, combining the pasta with the tomatoes and vinaigrette as soon as the pasta is done.
- Pasta and Shrimp Salad: Use 3 cups of cherry tomatoes, 1 small onion, 8 ounces small pasta, and 8 ounces Oregon baby shrimp, adding the shrimp after tossing the other ingredients with the vinaigrette.

Tomato Avocado Salad

Serves 3 to 4

This is a workhorse sort of salad, one you can make on the fly almost without thinking about it. It is an excellent accompaniment to almost anything, from plain yogurt to shrimp tacos, roasted chicken, and grilled fish.

3 cups chopped tomatoes or quartered cherry tomatoes
3 garlic cloves, crushed and minced
3 tablespoons minced red onion
1 large firm-ripe avocado, diced
Kosher salt
Juice of ½ lemon or lime
Black pepper in a mill
3 tablespoons extra-virgin olive oil
2 tablespoons chopped fresh Italian parsley, cilantro, or basil

Put the tomatoes into a medium bowl, add the garlic and red onion, and toss gently.

Add the avocado, season with salt and citrus, and toss very gently so as not to break up or mash the avocado. Season with several turns of black pepper, add the olive oil and herbs, and toss again.

Serve within 30 minutes.

Insalata Caprese
with Burrata

Serves 4 to 6

Burrata, nearly unheard of in the United States a decade ago, is a relatively new Italian cheese, with a history that goes back a few decades, not centuries. At its best, it is a thin sheet of mozzarella that encloses heavy cream and little mozzarella shards. It is delicate and fragile, with a very short shelf life. There are domestic versions now and many have an interior closer to ricotta than cheese and cream. If you can get the real thing, you should. If not, domestic burrata is pretty good.

1 burrata, 8 ounces
4 or 6 small (2-inch) tomatoes, preferably mixed colors, cored
Small handful cherry tomatoes, quartered
3 garlic cloves, crushed and minced
6 to 8 basil leaves, torn into small pieces
3 tablespoons extra-virgin olive oil
Flake salt
Black pepper in a mill
Basil sprigs, for garnish

Set the burrata off center on a large plate.

Cut each tomato into 6 wedges, cutting through the poles, not the equator. Scatter the tomatoes, randomly, on the plate. Add the cherry tomatoes.

Scatter the garlic over the tomatoes, followed by the basil.

Drizzle with olive oil, season with salt and pepper, garnish with basil sprigs, and serve.

Traditional Insalata Caprese

Serves 3 to 4

Insalata Caprese is never better than when it is made at the peak of tomato season and that is, indeed, the only time I make it or eat it. Enjoy it at its rightful time and then long for it when basil and tomatoes are not in season where you live.

8 ounces fresh mozzarella, well chilled
3 to 4 medium ripe summer tomatoes, cored
2 garlic cloves, crushed and minced
Flake salt
3 tablespoons best-quality extra-virgin olive oil
12 fresh basil leaves
Black pepper in a mill

Use a very thin, very sharp knife to cut the mozzarella into ⅜-inch-thick slices. Set aside briefly.

Cut the tomatoes into ⅜-inch rounds.

Arrange the tomatoes and mozzarella in circles on a large serving platter or individual plates. Scatter the garlic on top and season lightly with salt.

Drizzle with olive oil, tuck basil leaves here and there, and season with several turns of black pepper.

Let rest for 15 minutes, sprinkle with a bit more salt, and serve.

Tomatoes
with Sweet Onions and Sardines

Serves 4

The culinary possibilities of sardines, tiny, soft-boned members of the herring family named for the island of Sardinia where they were first canned, are often overlooked. Not only are they delicious, they are also an excellent source of calcium, protein, and beneficial omega-3 fatty acids. Here they add a light yet highly nutritious and delicious element to the simple tomato salad.

4 large tomatoes, sliced into ¼-inch rounds
1 small sweet onion, peeled and cut into very thin rounds
3 to 4 ounces canned sardines, drained
1 or 2 lemon wedges
Extra-virgin olive oil
Flake salt
Black pepper in a mill

Arrange the sliced tomatoes on one large or four individual plates, alternating them with rounds of onion.

Taking care not to break the sardines, remove them from their can if you have not already done so. Drain off the liquid or oil and scatter on top of the tomatoes and onions.

Squeeze lemon over the salad, drizzle with olive oil, and season with salt and pepper.

Let rest 15 minutes before serving.

Farm Market Salad

Serves 12 to 14

This salad is a more elaborate version of a simple sliced tomato salad, one I make throughout tomato season, especially when I am serving more than a few people. This salad presents an ideal opportunity to combine as many colors of tomatoes as you can find in your garden or at your local farmers market.

10 medium or large slicing tomatoes, a mix of red, orange, yellow, and green, trimmed and cut into ¼-inch rounds
3 small fresh sweet peppers of various colors, stemmed, seeded, and cut into very thin rounds
3 medium lemon cucumbers, trimmed and cut into very thin rounds
2 torpedo onions, cut into very thin rounds
5 small tomatoes, about 1½ inches in diameter, a mix of colors, cut into wedges
2 cups mixed cherry tomatoes, quartered
6 cloves garlic, peeled and minced
Flake salt
Black pepper in a mill
⅓ to ½ cup best-quality extra-virgin olive oil
6 ounces Dry Jack or similar cheese, grated or shaved
Several currant tomato sprigs, red and yellow
Handful of fresh basil leaves, plus several basil flowers, preferably opal basil

Arrange the sliced tomatoes on a very large nonreactive platter, alternating colors; start on the outside of the platter, creating several concentric circles. Tuck the peppers and cucumbers here and there between the tomatoes. Add a ring of onion slices on top of the second outer ring of tomatoes.

Scatter the small wedges of tomatoes on top of the salad, randomly, followed by the cherry tomatoes. Scatter the garlic over everything.

Season generously with salt and pepper and drizzle with olive oil. Scatter the cheese on top and add sprigs of currant tomatoes here and there, followed by basil and basil flower.

Cover with plastic wrap and let rest for 1 hour before serving.

Variation:

- Omit the grated cheese. Cut 8 ounces of mozzarella fresca into thin rounds and tuck them here and there between the tomatoes before adding other ingredients. Continue as directed in the main recipe.

Lakeville Tabbouleh

Serves 6 to 8

For several years, I lived in a southern corner of Sonoma County in the low, rolling hills of the dairy country known as Lakeville. It was a quiet time in the county then, with a population about 15 percent of what it is now. My young daughters thrived in the wide open hills and pastures, and I gardened as much as possible. My most successful crop was beautifully tender spinach. This tabbouleh was one of our staples.

1 cup bulgur wheat, rinsed under warm water, drained
¾ cup extra-virgin olive oil
½ cup fresh-squeezed lemon juice
2 teaspoons kosher salt, plus more to taste
Black pepper in a mill
1 bunch Italian parsley, stems discarded, chopped

1 bunch fresh young spinach, rinsed thoroughly, large stems discarded, cut into thin crosswise slices
2 cucumbers, peeled, seeded, and cut into small dice
4 celery stalks, cut into small dice
6 large ripe red tomatoes, skinned, seeded, and chopped
Plain yogurt or feta cheese

Put the dry bulgur in a large porcelain bowl and pour the olive oil and lemon juice over it. Add the salt and a few turns of black pepper and stir the mixture briefly. Scatter the parsley on top of the bulgur and spread the spinach on top of it. Add the cucumbers and celery and top with the tomatoes.

Cover the bowl tightly with a lid or plastic wrap and refrigerate for 24 hours.

Remove the salad from the refrigerator and gently toss it, being sure to pull up the bulgur from the bottom of the bowl and mix it thoroughly but gently with the other ingredients.

Serve immediately, with yogurt or feta alongside.

The tabbouleh will keep 2 or 3 days in the refrigerator but has the best flavor when eaten the first day.

Bread Salad
with Cherry Tomatoes, Sausage & Chimichurri

Serves 4 to 6

While I was promoting my book Vinaigrettes and Other Dressings (Harvard Common Press, 2013, $16.95), I typically took two or three dishes from the book with me, especially if I was at a farmers market. Bread salad is an easy dish to make on the spot and so it was often what I chose. I got into the habit of dressing it with the called-for vinaigrette and also topping it with a dollop of Chermoula, a moderately spicy Moroccan condiment. It was so popular and I sold so many books because of it that I now typically top my bread salads with either Chermoula or another fresh condiment. Here, I use Chimichurri, a dish as ubiquitous in Argentina as Chermoula is in Morocco. There are several versions of Chimichurri, some that include fresh tomatoes, which is what I use here.

½ cup Red Chimichurri (page 251)
4 cups cubed rustic hearth bread, about 2 days old
2 cups quartered cherry tomatoes, preferably a mix of colors
1 small red onion, cut into small dice
3 to 4 garlic cloves, crushed and minced
3 moderately spicy sausages, such as Moroccan merguez, Spanish chorizo, or andouille, cooked
Kosher salt
3 tablespoons fresh-squeezed lemon juice
2 or 3 pinches of crushed red pepper flakes
⅔ cup extra-virgin olive oil
Black pepper in a mill
½ cup chopped fresh Italian parsley leaves
¼ cup chopped fresh cilantro leaves

Make the Chimichurri if you have not already done so; set aside.

Put the bread into a large bowl, add the cherry tomatoes, red onion, and garlic, and toss gently.

Cut the sausages into thin rounds, cut the rounds in half, and add to the bowl. Season with salt and toss again.

Put the lemon juice, crushed red pepper flakes, and olive oil into a small bowl, add a generous pinch of salt and several turns of black pepper, and toss. Season with several turns of black pepper.

Pour the dressing over the salad and use two forks to toss throughly. Add the parsley and cilantro and toss again.

Serve within the hour with the Chimichurri alongside so that guests can top their salads with a generous dollop.

Variation:
- If you keep whole lemons in your freezer, grate one (while still frozen) and add it to the salad with the parsley and cilantro. It adds a remarkably yummy quality. There is no need to peel or seed the lemon; indeed, *you shouldn't.*

Greek-Inspired Bread Salad

Serves 3 to 4

This dish is inspired by fattoush, a Middle Eastern bread salad that uses toasted pita and sumac or za'atar, a blend of sumac and toasted and ground sesame seeds. Both are widely available in the United States, at speciality spice shops.

3 or 4 stale pitas or 4 slices stale hearth bread, in bite-sized pieces, lightly toasted (see Note on next page)
1 small shallot, minced
2 garlic cloves, minced
1 tablespoon freshly squeezed lemon juice
1 teaspoon best-quality white wine vinegar
1 teaspoon dried oregano
½ teaspoon ground sumac or za'atar, optional
Kosher salt
Black pepper in a mill
3 tablespoons extra-virgin olive oil
3 medium heirloom tomatoes, cored, halved (through the equator), and cut into wedges
½ small red onion, peeled and cut into thin lengthwise slices
1 small cucumber, peeled, seeded, and cut into thin half moons
½ cup green olives, pitted and sliced lengthwise
2 teaspoons capers
4 ounces feta cheese, broken into chunks
2 generous handfuls of small-leafed arugula

Put the bread into a wide, shallow bowl and set it aside.

Put the shallot and garlic into a small bowl, add the lemon juice, vinegar, oregano, and sumac or za'atar, if using, and season with salt and pepper. Set aside for about 15 minutes, while you prepare the vegetables.

Pour the olive oil into the shallot mixture, taste, and correct for salt, pepper, and acid balance.

Pour the dressing over the bread and toss.

Add the tomatoes, onion, cucumber, olives, capers, and cheese and toss again. Let rest for 10 minutes.

Put the arugula in a bowl, season with salt, and toss. Divide among individual bowls or plates. Top with the salad and serve.

> **NOTE**
> If you do not have stale bread, tear or cut fresh bread (either pita or hearth) into bite-sized pieces and toast it in a slow oven, turning it now and then, until it is lightly browned and crunchy.

Winter Bread Salad

Serves 4

There are countless ways to make bread salad without tomatoes, which is what you should do when they are not in season. But should you want a bit of tomato flavor in the dead of winter, use dried tomatoes.

Red Wine Vinaigrette (recipe follows)
4 cups cubed rustic hearth bread, about 2 days old
4 tablespoons dried-tomato bits
3 tablespoons capers, drained
1 small red onion, cut into small dice
4 cloves garlic, crushed and minced
1 cup black olives of choice, pitted and chopped
½ cup minced fresh Italian parsley

Make the vinaigrette and set it aside briefly.

Put the bread and dried-tomato bits into a large bowl, add half the vinaigrette, and toss. Set aside for 30 minutes.

Add the capers, onion, garlic, olives, and parsley and toss again.

Add the remaining dressing, transfer to a serving bowl, cover, and let rest 20 to 30 minutes before serving.

Red Wine Vinaigrette

Makes about 1 cup

1 shallot, minced
Kosher salt
Pinch of ground allspice
3 tablespoons red wine vinegar
1 tablespoon fresh lemon juice
2 teaspoons minced fresh oregano
1 teaspoon minced fresh thyme
⅔ cup extra-virgin olive oil
Black pepper in a mill

Put the shallot into a small bowl, add a generous pinch or two of salt and the allspice, pour the vinegar and lemon juice over it, and let rest 15 minutes. Add the oregano, thyme, and olive oil. Taste, correct for salt, and season with several turns of black pepper.

Breads, Sandwiches, Pizza & Pie

Who invented the sandwich? Although the discovery is credited to John Montagu, the fourth Earl of Sandwich (1718–1792), I suspect that it was much earlier than the earl's legendary evenings at the gambling table that a man or woman first folded a piece of bread around a savory ingredient or two. The naming of the concoction, that's a matter for the early marketers, and someone apparently sensed the catchy appeal of the earl's district.

Regardless of its origins, the sandwich is firmly entrenched in the culinary practices of numerous cultures, none more so perhaps than here in the United States, where it remains in its diverse forms the single most common lunch item. And a slice or two of tomato graces the majority of our sandwiches year-round, regardless of the season. Fast-food hamburgers automatically come with tomatoes unless you request otherwise. Then, of course, there's turkey on whole-wheat with lettuce and tomato: so essential, and with its ingredients so linked together they are nearly a single item. This ubiquitous form is not, however, the best use of the tomato between two slices of bread. For the sandwich's finest moment, one needs to look to summer, to gardens full of sun-warmed tomatoes, and to the best bread you can find.

One could say that summer is a tomato sandwich. The essence of all that is good about the leisurely season is distilled in the simple, compelling combination of bread, tomato, and salt. The silky texture, like liquid sunlight; the sweetness and the slight burst of acidity; the way the juices sink down into the bread. At no other time of year is this elemental pleasure ours except in the languid days of summer's heat. Don't let summer pass without having your fill of its simplest pleasure.

Americans love sandwiches, in part because we tend to eat on the go—in the car or on foot or whatever mode of transportation—nearly anywhere that it is not forbidden. Although it is not my favorite way of

dining—I prefer a stationary rather than a mobile meal—I thoroughly appreciate a great sandwich, especially one that involves summer tomatoes.

These variations on one of our country's favorite culinary themes build on the concept of the simple summer tomato sandwich in a variety of delicious ways. Do keep in mind that a sandwich will not be better than the bread it is built upon. Use the best available to you, and if that's not good enough, make your own. Few things are as pleasantly therapeutic as the baking of bread.

Savory Scones with Sage & Tomato Butter
Popovers with Dried Tomatoes

Summer Tomato Sandwich, Version 1
Summer Tomato Sandwich, Version 2
Summer Tomato Sandwich, Version 3
Roasted Tomato Sandwich
Bacon, Lettuce & Tomato Sandwich
Grilled Cheese & Summer Tomato Sandwich
Focaccia with Cherry Tomatoes
Focaccia Sandwich with Tuna Mayonnaise, Eggs & Tomatoes
Focaccia Sandwich Niçoise

Tomato Bread Pudding

Pizza in America
Pizza Margherita
Grilled Pizzas with Tomato Concassé, Mozzarella & Farm Eggs

Summer Tomato Pie with Fresh Basil, with Two Variations
Tomato Galette with Bacon
Savory Galette Dough

Savory Scones
with Sage & Tomato Butter

Makes 8 to 12 scones

The secret to tender scones is to have the butter well chilled and to not overmix the ingredients.

¾ cup whole milk or half-and-half
¼ cup dried-tomato bits
2 cups flour
1 tablespoon baking powder
½ teaspoon salt
5 tablespoons butter, chilled and cut into ¼-inch pieces

1 egg, beaten
2 tablespoons minced fresh sage leaves
¾ cup grated Dry Jack cheese
12 perfect sage leaves
Heavy cream

Place a baking sheet in the oven and preheat to 450°F.

In a small bowl, pour the milk over the dried-tomato bits and let sit for 30 minutes. Mix together the flour, baking powder, and salt. Add the butter and, using either your fingertips or a pastry blender, quickly work it into the flour mixture so that it has the consistency of bread crumbs. Stir the egg and sage into the milk and dried tomatoes. Make a well in the center of the flour mixture, pour the milk in, and mix lightly and quickly with a fork until it forms a loose, soft dough. Add the cheese, blend quickly with your fingers, and turn the dough out onto a lightly floured surface. Knead very gently for 30 seconds.

Using a rolling pin or patting with the palm of your hand, spread out the dough into a rectangle ¼ inch thick. Using a sharp knife, cut into 8 to 12 triangles. Brush the surface of each scone with the heavy cream and then very lightly press a sage leaf into the center of each scone. Brush with a little more cream if necessary to make the leaf stay in place.

Using a spatula, transfer the scones to the hot baking sheet and bake until lightly golden, about 10 minutes. Remove from the oven and transfer immediately to a rack to cool slightly.

Serve warm with Tomato Butter (page 250) or Spicy Tomato Jelly (page 256).

A Tomato Cookbook

Popovers
with Dried Tomatoes

Makes about 1 dozen popovers

A popover rising all golden and fragrant out of its tin is a delightful sight and one that offers a simple but satisfying sense of accomplishment. Popovers are welcome at breakfast but are also delicious at dinner, alongside roast beef, roast pork, and roast chicken.

1⅓ cups milk, room temperature
1 tablespoon melted butter
1⅓ cups all-purpose flour
⅓ cup sun-dried tomato bits
1 tablespoon finely minced fresh
    Italian parsley

½ teaspoon kosher salt
3 eggs, room temperature
¾ cup Fontina cheese
Tomato Butter (page 250)

Have heavy, deep tins (cast iron works best) buttered and the oven preheated to 450°F.

Heat the milk and butter together over medium heat. When the butter is melted, add the flour, tomato bits, parsley, and salt, and beat vigorously with a wooden spoon until the mixture comes together and pulls away from the side of the pan.

Remove from the heat immediately.

Add the eggs, one at a time, beating well after each addition but not overbeating; stop when each egg is fully incorporated into the mixture.

Spoon just enough of the popover batter into each muffin tin to completely coat the bottom. Divide the cheese among the 12 popovers and then fill each tin about one-half to two-thirds full with the remaining batter. Bake immediately and after 15 minutes reduce the heat to 325°F. Bake for another 15 to 30 minutes until the outsides of the popovers are firm and the tops golden. Remove them from the oven and serve immediately, with a tomato butter alongside.

Summer Tomato Sandwich
Version 1

Serves 1, easily doubled

Invariably, I make this sandwich immediately upon the discovery of the first tomatoes of the season. I never grow tired of it, and think of it longingly as I await the first of the harvest.

Homemade or best-quality commercial mayonnaise
2 slices of your favorite bread (I prefer thick, sourdough hearth bread),
    lightly toasted
1 medium garden tomato, stem end removed, sliced into ¼-inch-thick rounds
Flake salt
Black pepper in a mill

Spread a generous amount of mayonnaise over both pieces of bread. Set the slices of tomato on top of the mayonnaise. Season the tomatoes with salt and pepper, add the top slice, and enjoy.

Summer Tomato Sandwich
Version 2

Serves 4

This sandwich is only slightly more complex than a simple tomato sandwich, and it's bright with the flavors of sweet basil and onions, two of summer's other delights.

8 slices of thick, country-style bread, lightly toasted
Homemade or best-quality commerical mayonnaise
4 garden tomatoes, stem end removed, sliced ¼ inch thick
1 medium or 2 small sweet onions, peeled and cut into thin rounds
Flake salt
Black pepper in a mill
Several leaves of fresh basil

Set the toasted bread on your work surface and slather each piece with a generous amount of mayonnaise. Tile tomatoes on 4 slices of the bread and season with salt and pepper.

Top the tomatoes with basil leaves followed by onion.

Top with the remaining slices of bread and serve immediately.

Summer Tomato Sandwich
Version 3

Makes 4 sandwiches

I prefer this sandwich on whole-wheat sourdough hot dog buns, which are the perfect shape for nestling all the ingredients. If they are not available, your favorite bread will do.

4 whole-wheat hot dog buns, opened and very lightly toasted
2 large or 3 medium garden tomatoes, trimmed and cut into thin rounds
2 medium lemon cucumbers, unpeeled and thinly sliced
1 small red onion, thinly sliced
Flake salt
3 or 4 garlic cloves, minced
Extra-virgin olive oil
Black pepper in a mill
16 fresh basil leaves

Set the buns or bread on your work surface.

Cut the sliced tomatoes in half and tuck them into the buns. Cut the cucumbers in half and add them alongside the tomatoes. Add the onion.

Season lightly with salt.

Scatter garlic on top, drizzle with olive oil, and season with black pepper. Tuck basil leaves here and there and enjoy immediately.

Variation:
- Add 2 or 3 thin slices of soppressata into each bun before adding the vegetables.

Roasted Tomato Sandwich

Serves 4 to 6

If you grow tomatoes, I recommend keeping roasted tomatoes in the refrigerator during their season. They are perfect for a fast meal and can be turned into a sauce very quickly. Here, they create one of the simplest sandwiches imaginable and it's a real treat—bright, refreshing, and full of the essence of summer. It is, by the way, a rather messy sandwich, so be prepared for lots of dripping and oozing out the sides. If such a mess does not appeal to you, simply serve the sandwiches open-faced.

4 large or 8 medium garden tomatoes, ripe or very ripe
1 tablespoon extra-virgin olive oil
3 cloves garlic, minced
1 fresh sourdough baguette, cut into 4 pieces, each split in half
Flake salt
Black pepper in a mill
Handful of basil leaves, thinly sliced, or 2 tablespoons snipped chives

Roast the tomatoes several hours before using so that they have time to cool. To do so, preheat the oven to 300°F. Peel the tomatoes, cut off the stem ends, and place them in a shallow baking dish. Drizzle the olive oil over the tomatoes and turn to coat them; scatter the garlic on top of the tomatoes. Bake until the tomatoes are very soft and begin to brown, about 40 minutes. Drain off any juices that form every 20 minutes or so (save them for soup, stock, or vinaigrette) so that the tomatoes roast nearly dry rather than stew in their juices. Remove them from the oven, allow them to cool, and refrigerate, covered, until ready to use.

To assemble the sandwiches, toast, grill, or broil the baguette until golden and slightly crisp.

Spread several spoonfuls of the roasted tomatoes on the bottom piece of the bread, pressing them in as much as possible. Season with salt and pepper, scatter the basil or chives on top, and add the top half of the bread.

Variations:

- Before adding the tomato, rub both pieces of bread with several cut cloves of garlic.

- Toss the tomatoes with a minced jalapeño or serrano before roasting them. Top with cilantro instead of basil or chives.

A Tomato Cookbook

Bacon, Lettuce & Tomato Sandwich

Serves 1, easily doubled

The year's first BLT is one of my most beloved rituals and I always wait until really good tomatoes are available where I live. In the first edition of this book, I included several variations on the classic theme but I have removed them from this new edition. In 2003, my book The BLT Cookbook *(Morrow) collected those and many others, along with pastas, salads, risottos, and more that celebrate the trinity of ingredients. That same year, I built the World's Biggest BLT at the Kendall-Jackson Tomato Festival and have, since then, repeated the giant sandwich on several occasions. The book is currently out of print but I am hoping it, too, will be reissued sometime soon, as everyone loves a BLT in one form or another.*

In the meantime, this is my celebratory version, the one that launches the season. When making the sandwich, please observe certain rules for the very best results. First, the bread should be lightly toasted. If you toast it too much, it may cut the roof of your mouth; if you don't toast it enough, it may fall apart. Second, the bacon must have snap, which means it shouldn't be too thick and must be cooked until it is fully crisp. Tomatoes must not be sliced too thin or too thick; ⅜-inch rounds are perfect. For the first BLT of the year, use Best Foods/Hellmann's mayonnaise or it won't have the right flavor. The mayonnaise must be slathered on in one light, fast stroke; do not rub it into the bread. You must use the outer leaves of iceberg lettuce; inner leaves are a bit cabbage-y. Finally, season the tomatoes with kosher or other flake salt and assemble the ingredients in the exact order I describe.

2 slices center-cut sourdough hearth bread, lightly toasted
3 tablespoons Best Foods/Hellmann's brand mayonnaise, plus more to taste
2 small full-flavored ripe tomatoes, cut into ⅜-inch-thick rounds
Flake salt
3 to 4 bacon slices, fried until completely crisp, drained
3 or 4 small outer leaves of iceberg lettuce

Set the lightly toasted bread on a clean work surface and slather both pieces with mayonnaise, using as much as you like.

Tile the tomatoes on top of the bottom slice of the bread, overlapping them enough so that there is room for 5 to 6 slices. Season somewhat generously with salt.

Stack the bacon on top of the tomatoes.

Set the lettuce on top of the bacon, tearing it as necessary so that it fits. Season lightly with salt.

Set the top piece of bread on the sandwich and enjoy immediately.

Repeat until the first fall frost.

Grilled Cheese &
Summer Tomato Sandwich

Serves 2

The best Cheddar cheese—Montgomery Cheddar from England, for example—is crumbly; you can't grate it or slice it successfully and you shouldn't even try, as it is best appreciated neat, on its own. For the comfort of a grilled cheese sandwich, you need something pedestrian and inexpensive; it is part of the alchemy. If you're on the mend from a summer cold or there's been a cold snap, you know what to do: serve the sandwiches with tomato soup. Other cheeses work well in this sandwich, too, especially Jack, Italian Fontina, and goat milk Cheddar.

4 slices bread of choice (I prefer sourdough hearth bread)
Best-quality mayonnaise, optional
Dijon mustard, optional
1 small summer tomato, trimmed and cut into ⅜-inch rounds
Kosher salt
6 to 8 ounces cheddar cheese of choice, grated
Worcestershire sauce
Bottled hot sauce
1 tablespoon butter, plus more as needed

Set the bread on a clean work surface and quickly smear mayonnaise or mustard or both over each slice. Be as generous as you like and add the condiments in one sweep of a knife or thin rubber spatula; do not rub either into the bread.

Spread tomatoes on 2 slices of bread, season with a little salt, and top with cheese.

Sprinkle a little Worcestershire sauce and hot sauce over the cheese. Top with the second slices of bread.

Set a sauté pan that will hold both sandwiches over medium heat, add about half the butter, and, when it is melted, add the sandwiches. Cook for about 3 minutes, until the bread is golden brown. Quickly add the remaining butter, lift out the sandwiches, and, when the butter melts, turn them over into the pan. Set a heavy lid directly on top of the sandwiches and cook another 3 minutes or so, until the bread is golden brown and the cheese is completely melted.

Transfer to sturdy napkins or plates and enjoy immediately.

Focaccia
with Cherry Tomatoes

Serves 4 to 6

When I wrote the first edition of this book, focaccia was not widely available unless you lived where there was a good Italian bakery. Now, it is almost everywhere and so I removed the recipe for making it from scratch. Enjoy this rustic open-faced sandwich whenever cherry tomatoes are abundant.

¼ sheet (9 x 13 inches) of focaccia, warmed in the oven
2 cups cherry tomatoes, halved
2 tablespoons extra-virgin olive oil
Flake salt
Black pepper in a mill
Several basil leaves, cut into very thin strips

Cut the focaccia into pieces and set on a serving platter.

Put the tomatoes into a small bowl, add the olive oil, season with salt and pepper, and toss gently. Spoon the tomatoes onto each piece of focaccia, scatter basil on top, and serve immediately.

A Tomato Cookbook

Focaccia Sandwich
with Tuna Mayonnaise, Eggs & Tomatoes

Makes 4 large sandwiches

The technique you use for mixing the tuna and olive oil—either in a processor or by hand—will have an important impact on your final result. If you prefer a coarser, more rustic effect, mix by hand. For a smooth, more delicate taste and texture, use a processor. This sandwich, as well as the one that follows, makes great picnic fare. Be sure to wrap each sandwich tightly in plastic wrap and keep it chilled. A bowl of olives is a perfect accompaniment to this hearty, flavorful sandwich.

1 can (6½ ounces) imported canned tuna
2 cloves garlic, crushed and minced
½ cup extra-virgin olive oil, plus up to ¼ cup
Flake salt
Black pepper in a mill
½ sheet focaccia
2 garden tomatoes, ends removed, sliced ¼ inch thick
2 hard-cooked farm eggs, sliced into thin rounds

In a food processor or by hand, beat together the tuna, garlic, and olive oil until a thick, mayonnaise-like sauce forms. Add additional olive oil, up to ¼ cup more, if necessary, to reach the desired consistency. Taste and season with salt and pepper.

The mayonnaise may be made a day or two in advance; store in the refrigerator until ready to use.

Cut the focaccia into 8 equal pieces and spread a generous amount of the mayonnaise on 4 pieces.

Top with sliced tomato and egg, season with salt and pepper, and add the second slices of bread.

Serve immediately or wrap tightly and refrigerate until ready to use.

Focaccia Sandwich Niçoise

Makes 4 sandwiches

When you combine the anchovies, tuna, garlic, and olives with olive oil you are basically making tuna tapenade mayonnaise. It is rich, bold, and delicious. This is one of my favorite picnic items, and I particularly like it when it has been made several hours earlier and the flavors have had time to mingle.

8 anchovy fillets, 4 soaked in
    1 tablespoon of red wine vinegar
1 can (6½ ounces) imported tuna,
    drained
3 large cloves garlic, peeled
1 tablespoon minced fresh Italian
    parsley
¾ cup Niçoise or California black
    olives, pitted

⅔ cup extra-virgin olive oil
½ sheet focaccia
6 to 8 small new potatoes, boiled
    until tender, thinly sliced
Flake salt
2 hard-boiled eggs, sliced
2 garden tomatoes, trimmed and cut
    into ¼-inch-thick rounds
1 cup thinly shredded cabbage

Place 4 of the anchovy fillets (reserve the ones in vinegar), tuna, garlic, parsley, and olives in a food processor. Pulse until almost smooth. With the machine operating, slowly drizzle in the olive oil. Transfer to a medium bowl. Use right away or cover and refrigerate for up to 2 days.

Drain the vinegar off the remaining anchovies.

Cut the focaccia into 8 equal pieces and spread a generous amount of the tapenade mayonnaise over 4 slices. Top with sliced potatoes and season lightly with salt. Add egg slices and season with a bit of salt and several turns of black pepper.

Add the tomato and top each sandwich with an anchovy fillet and add the shredded cabbage.

Brush the remaining pieces of bread with a little mayonnaise and invert onto the sandwiches.

Serve immediately or wrap and chill until ready to serve.

Tomato Bread Pudding

Serves 6 to 8

Bread pudding is a lovely fall dish, when evenings are cold but there are still local tomatoes. Serve it with roasted chicken and a big green salad.

5 or 6 bacon slices

4 cups sourdough hearth bread of choice, torn into bite-sized pieces

3 dead-ripe tomatoes, cored and chopped

½ cup chopped fresh Italian parsley leaves

3 ounces grated cheese, such as Gruyère, Fontina, Parmigiano-Reggiano, or Dry Jack

3 farm eggs, beaten

2 cups whole milk

½ cup heavy cream

2 tablespoons double-concentrated tomato paste

3 garlic cloves, pressed

Kosher salt

Black pepper in a mill

Fry the bacon until it is crisp and transfer it to absorbent paper to drain.

Put the bread into a large mixing bowl and drizzle the bacon drippings over it. Toss to distribute evenly.

Add the tomatoes, parsley, and cheese, toss well, and season with salt and several generous turns of black pepper. Set aside.

Combine the eggs, milk, cream, tomato paste, and pressed garlic and whisk until smooth. Season with salt and pepper.

Tip the bread mixture into a baking dish, such as a 2-quart soufflé dish. Pour the custard over it, agitate the dish gently to distribute it evenly, cover with aluminum foil, and set aside.

Preheat the oven to 325°F and set the bread pudding on the middle rack of the oven. Cook for 15 minutes, increase the heat to 425°F, and cook for 10 to 15 minutes more, until the top is puffed up and lightly browned.

Remove from the oven and let rest for 10 to 15 minutes before serving.

A Tomato Cookbook   **161**

Pizza in America

Neapolitan Pizza is everywhere these days, made by pizzaioli who train in Naples and receive official certification.

The thin-crusted pizzas they make, using Italian 00 flour and very few toppings, are relatively new to Americans, popularized in the last decade or so by restaurants such as A16 in San Francisco and Keste in New York's West Village.

These pizzas are not weighted down by the thick tomato sauce typical of American-style pizzas. Some have such a light brushing of tomato concassé and olive oil and many have no tomato sauce at all. They are tender and chewy.

If you enjoy making pizza at home, get some Italian 00 flour and invest in a sturdy pizza tile for your oven.

PIZZA DOUGH

MAKES 1 12-INCH PIZZA SKIN

2 teaspoons active dry yeast
¼ cup warm water
3 cups flour, preferably Italian 00 flour, plus more for dusting
1 teaspoon kosher salt
4 teaspoons extra virgin olive oil, plus more as needed
Corn meal

Put the yeast and warm water into a large mixing bowl and set aside for ten minute. Stir in ½ cup flour, the salt, and the olive oil.
Add more flour, ½ cup at a time, until you have about ½ cup remaining.
Dust a clean work surface and turn out the dough onto it. Gently knead the dough until it is smooth and velvet; it will take about 7 minutes. Sprinkle with flour as needed if the dough becomes sticky.
Rinse and dry the mixing bowl and coat the inside with olive oil. Set the dough in the bowl, cover with a damp tea towel, set in a warm part of the room, and let rise for 2 hours, until the dough has doubled in size.
Gently turn the dough out onto a clean floured surface, cover and let rest 5 minutes. Using the heel of your hand, press the dough out flat. Pick it up with both hands and stretch it into a 12-inch circle. Alternately, use a rolling pin to roll lit into a circle.
Sprinkle a pizza paddle or thin wooden cutting board with corn meal, set the skin on it, add toppings, and bake according to directions in the recipe.

Pizza Margherita

Makes 2 10- to 12-inch pizzas

This classic pizza of Naples sports the colors of the Italian flag: tomato red, basil green, and the silky white of melted mozzarella. It was named for Queen Margherita, who presided over Italy after unification and the development of the tricolored flag.

1 recipe pizza dough, page 162
6 tablespoons extra-virgin olive oil
8 ounces mozzarella fresca, sliced
Handful whole fresh basil leaves

4 to 6 medium ripe Roma tomatoes, cut in rounds
Flake salt
Black pepper in a mill

Preheat the oven, preferably with a pizza stone in place, to 500°F.

Cut the pizza dough in half and sprinkle a clean work surface lightly with flour. Roll out one piece of dough as thinly as possible; do not worry if it is not perfectly round.

Sprinkle a bit of flour on a pizza paddle or on an inverted half-sheet pan.

Drizzle half the oil over it, top with half the cheese and half the basil leaves, and arrange the tomatoes on top. Season lightly with salt and pepper.

Carefully transfer the pizza to the pizza stone and cook for about 6 minutes. Check on the pizza and continue to cook until the edge of the dough is puffed and lightly browned. Remove from the oven, set on a rack, and repeat with the second dough.

Transfer the finished pizza to a clean work surface, cut in wedges, and enjoy.

Grilled Pizzas
with Tomato Concassé, Mozzarella & Farm Eggs

Serves 4

Grilling pizza became a very popular way to entertain in California about a decade or so ago. Sometimes, the host provides the doughs, always shaped to size, and a huge array of toppings and guests construct their own. Adding an egg to pizza became trendy right about the same time and for good reason; it is delicious, especially when you use good farm eggs. You'll need a grill with a lid; if you don't have one, simply omit the eggs.

2 8- to 10-inch rounds of pizza
    dough, page 162
3 tablespoons extra-virgin olive oil
1½ cups Tomato Concassé (page 263)
4 to 5 garlic cloves, minced
Kosher salt

Black pepper in a mill
8 ounces mozzarella fresca, thinly
    sliced
4 large farm eggs
Crushed red pepper flakes

Prepare the pizza dough.

Build a fire in an outdoor grill and wait until the coals are completely covered in ash and have passed their hottest point.

Cut the dough in quarters and use your hands to slowly stretch each piece into a roundish disk. Grill the stretched doughs over direct heat until the dough becomes firm and is lightly toasted, about 1 to 2 minutes.

Working quickly, transfer the pizzas to a work surface near the grill, setting the cooked side down. Drizzle or brush olive oil over the surface, spread Tomato Concassé on top, scatter garlic over the tomato, season with salt and pepper, and top with mozzarella.

Return to the grill and cook for 1 minute. Carefully break an egg on top of each pizza, cover, and cook until the egg is set, about 2 to 3 minutes, depending on the heat of the coals.

Remove from the heat, season lightly with salt, pepper, and crushed red pepper flakes, and enjoy right away.

Summer Tomato Pie
with Fresh Basil, with Two Variations

Serves 6

For the very best results, use dense-fleshed local tomatoes that are heavy for their size and drain off most of their juices, as described in the recipe. This will keep the biscuit-style pie crust from becoming mushy and will provide the most concentrated tomato flavor. Once you get the hang of it, this pie will likely become a summer staple; it is one of my most requested recipes ever. When I make it, I use a local cheese, either Joe Matos St. George, Bellwether Pepato, or Weirauch Carabiner. Whatever cheese you use should have good melting qualities.

2½ pounds medium ripe beefsteak tomatoes
Kosher salt
1½ cups all-purpose flour
1 tablespoon black peppercorns, cracked
1 tablespoon baking powder
6 tablespoons (3 ounces) butter, chilled and cut into ¼-inch cubes
½ cup whole milk
1 cup, lightly packed, basil leaves
Black pepper in a mill
2 cups (8 ounces) grated cheese, such as medium Cheddar or Monterey Jack
¾ cup mayonnaise, homemade or Best Foods brand
2 tablespoons freshly squeezed lemon juice
3 tablespoons heavy cream
Maldon salt flakes
Small basil sprigs, for garnish

First, prepare the tomatoes. Peel them by piercing them, one at a time, on the tines of a fork through the stem end. Hold the fork and rotate the tomatoes over a high gas flame or hot electric burner as the skin blisters; it should take about 30 seconds for each tomato.

When all of the tomatoes have been blistered, use your fingers to pull off the skins. Use a sharp paring knife to cut out the core and slice off both ends. Next, set a strainer over a medium bowl and hold a tomato over it; gently squeeze to release gel and seeds, using a finger to loosen seeds as necessary. Do not squeeze too hard; you want the tomatoes intact.

Set a platter near your work surface and cut each tomato into rounds not quite a quarter inch thick. Set the sliced tomatoes on the platter and season lightly with salt. Cover with a sheet of wax paper and set aside.

Press as much of the gel and juices through the strainer as possible and discard what remains. Pour the juices into a bowl or glass, cover, and refrigerate.

Next, make the pie dough.

Preheat the oven to 375°F.

Sift or mix together the flour, pepper, 1 teaspoon kosher salt, and baking powder. Either by hand using a pastry blender or in a food processor, quickly work the butter into the flour mixture so that it has the consistency of cornmeal. If using a food processor, add the milk, pulse quickly two or three times until the dough just barely comes together, and then turn out onto a floured surface. If working by hand, make a small well in the center of the flour, pour the milk in, and then mix quickly with a fork until the dough comes together but is still soft and sticky. Turn onto a floured surface.

Knead the dough for about 30 seconds and then let it rest for 10 minutes. Cut the dough in half, roll out one half to about 11 inches, and then carefully fit it into a 9-inch pie pan.

Transfer the tomatoes from the platter onto paper towels and tip any juices that have drained into the bowl or glass with the other collected juices. (Save the juices for another use or simply to enjoy chilled, with a squeeze of lemon or a splash of good vodka.)

Cover the bottom of the dough with a layer of tomatoes, overlapping them just slightly and using about a third of the tomatoes. Tuck about a third of the basil leaves here and there between the tomatoes, followed by a little salt and a few turns of black pepper. Top with about a third of the cheese. Add two more layers, ending with the last of the cheese.

Working quickly, combine the mayonnaise with the lemon juice and carefully spread it over the top of the pie.

Quickly roll out the reserved dough, fit it over the pie, and seal the edges by pinching them together. Cut several slits in the dough to allow steam to escape.

Brush the dough with the heavy cream and sprinkle lightly with Maldon salt flakes.

Bake for 40 minutes or until the crust is golden brown. Let rest for 15 minutes before serving. Cut in wedges and serve hot.

Variations:
- Instead of basil, use cilantro leaves. Thin the mayonnaise with lime juice and stir in 1 teaspoon chipotle powder. Garnish each slice with a cilantro sprig.
- Instead of basil, use ½ cup chopped (not minced) Italian parsley leaves and 6 to 8 slices of bacon, fried until crisp and then crumbled. Fix the parsley and bacon together and scatter over each layer of tomatoes. Garnish with small Italian parsley sprigs.

Tomato Galette with Bacon

Serves 4 to 6

Galettes are tarts with free-form dough. They are among the most delicious of all tarts and have the added benefit of being fairly easy to make. When students tell me they can't make dough, I use this recipe to teach them how. Because it is so easy, it boosts confidence quickly and I've found over the years that it's mostly lack of confidence that gets in the way of making good dough. As long as you use chilled butter and cold water and don't overwork the mixture, you should have excellent results every time.

In these savory galettes, use tomatoes that are heavy for their size and ripe but not quite dead ripe.

3 to 4 medium, dense-fleshed heirloom tomatoes
Kosher salt
4 strips bacon
14-inch galette dough, recipe follows, chilled for 1 hour
3 ounces Italian Fontina or similar cheese, thinly sliced
Black pepper in a mill
2 tablespoons fresh snipped chives or fresh minced Italian parsley
1 egg white, mixed with 1 tablespoon of water
1 teaspoon flake salt

Remove the stem cores of the tomatoes and slice off each end. Cut each tomato into 3/8-inch-thick round slices, season with salt, cover the slices with a tea towel, and set them aside.

Fry the bacon until it is just crisp; transfer to absorbent paper and set aside.

Drain the juices that have collected around the tomatoes, using your fingers to press out any large pockets of seeds and gel.

Preheat the oven to 400°F. Remove the chilled dough from the refrigerator and if you have not put it on a baking sheet lined with parchment, do so now.

Arrange the cheese over the surface of the tart, leaving a 2-inch margin around the edges. If more juices have formed around the tomatoes, drain them again and set the tomatoes on top of the cheese in concentric circles that overlap slightly. Season the tomatoes lightly with kosher salt and generously with black pepper from the mill. Scatter the chives over the top of the tomatoes, arrange the bacon strips on top, and then gently fold the edges of the tart up and over the tomatoes, pleating the edges as you fold them. Using a pastry brush, brush the edge of the tart lightly with the egg wash and sprinkle it with the sea salt or Hawaiian salt.

Bake until the pastry is golden brown and the tomatoes are soft and fragrant, about 35 to 40 minutes.

Transfer to a rack to cool, cut into wedges, and serve warm.

Variations:
- Vegetarians can simply omit the bacon.

- To make individual galettes, cut the dough into 8 equal pieces, roll them out, and fill according to the instructions in the main recipe, using 1 large slice of tomato per galette. Scatter a few quartered cherry tomatoes to each one.

- Omit the cheese; add a layer of very thinly sliced red onion before arranging the tomatoes.

Savory Galette Dough

Makes 2 large or 8 small galettes

2 cups (about 10 ounces) all-purpose flour
¾ teaspoon kosher salt
1 teaspoon freshly ground black pepper
6 ounces unsalted butter, cold
½ cup ice-cold water

In a medium bowl, combine the flour, salt, and the pepper. Cut in the butter, using your fingers or a pastry cutter, until the mixture resembles coarse cornmeal; work very quickly so that the butter does not warm. Add the ice water and press the dough gently until it just comes together; do not overmix—it's okay if there appears to be unmoistened flour. Spread a sheet of plastic wrap over a flat surface and turn the dough out onto it.

Grip the ends of the plastic wrap and pull them together, so that the wrap presses the dough together. Wrap the dough into a ball and refrigerate it for at least 30 minutes. (At this point, the dough can be wrapped a second time and stored in the freezer for up to 3 months.)

To make the pastry, cut the dough into 2 or 8 equal pieces, depending on whether you will make large or individual galettes.

Set the dough on a floured work surface and use the palm of your hand to pat it flat. Using a rolling pin, roll the dough into a circle about an eighth of an inch thick. Large galettes should be about 14 inches in diameter; small galettes should be about 6 to 8 inches in diameter.

Set the dough on a baking sheet covered with parchment paper and keep chilled until ready to fill. (The dough can also be frozen after it has been rolled; be sure to wrap it tightly.)

Pasta, Rice & Polenta

Few dishes are more iconic than spaghetti with marinara or a meaty tomato sauce. When we're just learning to talk, we call it "bisketti" or "skabetti" and many of us grew up eating it from a can, Franco-American Spaghettios, perhaps, or Chef Boyardee Spaghetti & Meatballs. My mother made it frequently, using ground beef, garlic powder, onion powder, and canned tomato sauce because she knew I would eat it. It remains one of my favorite comfort foods, especially cold, right out of the refrigerator, sometime after midnight.

This chapter does not feature those familiar pasta dishes. You'll find recipes for classic sauces in Classic & Contemporary Tomato Sauces (pages 261–280). Here, I highlight a few favorite preparations that are, for the most part, my own and not based on traditional dishes, though a few are inspired by the classics.

Pasta with Uncooked Summer Tomato Sauce, with Four Variations
Lucas's Favorite Pasta
Fresh Tomato Pasta with Butter & Basil
Linguine with Sautéed Tomatoes, Chèvre & Fresh Herbs
Linguine with Tomatoes, Oranges, Fennel, Currants & Olives
Tomato Pasta with Chicken, Olives & Dried-Tomato Cream Sauce
Macaroni & Cheese with Tomatoes & Pancetta
Pappardelle with Lamb Ragù
Tomato & Polenta Tart with Basil Mayonnaise
Meyer Lemon Risotto with Tomato Concassé
Hot Rice with Cool Tomatoes

Pasta
with Uncooked Summer Tomato Sauce, with Four Variations

Serves 3 to 4

One of the simple pleasures of summer is pasta with a flavorful sauce that does not require cooking. By the time the pasta itself is ready, you can have a fragrant sauce waiting for it. All you need is tomato concassé, made from ripe summer tomatoes, and whatever other seasonings you prefer. Here is a template recipe that serves up to four people, along with several variations.

Kosher salt
12 ounces strand pasta (spaghettini, spaghetti, linguine)
1½ cups Tomato Concassé (page 263)
2 garlic cloves, crushed and minced
½ cup chopped fresh basil leaves
⅓ cup extra-virgin olive oil
Black pepper in a mill
2 tablespoons butter or crème fraîche, optional

Fill a large pot two-thirds full with water, season generously with salt, and bring to a boil over high heat. When the water reaches a rolling boil, add the pasta and stir until the water returns to a boil. Adjust the heat so that the water does not boil over and cook the pasta, stirring now and then, according to package directions until just done.

Meanwhile, put the Tomato Concassé into a medium serving bowl, add the garlic and basil, and season with salt. Stir in the olive oil.

When the pasta is done, drain it but do not rinse it and immediately tip it into the bowl. Add the butter or crème fraîche, if using, and use two forks to lift the pasta over and over until it is evenly coated in the sauce. Taste, correct for salt and pepper, and serve immediately.

Variations:

- Use ½ cup julienned spearmint leaves in place of the basil.

- Add ¾ cup (3 ounces) cubed or crumbled feta cheese to the sauce immediately before adding the hot pasta.

- Mince 3 small anchovy fillets and add them to the tomatoes, along with 1 tablespoon red wine vinegar. Replace the basil with chopped fresh Italian parsley.

- Add ½ cup pitted and sliced picholine olives and ½ cup pitted and sliced Niçoise olives to the tomato sauce. Reduce the basil to 2 tablespoons and add 2 tablespoons chopped fresh Italian parsley and 2 tablespoons chopped fresh oregano.

Lucas's Favorite Pasta

Serves 2, easily doubled

My grandson Lucas was born with a subtle, eager, and adventurous palate and he loves my cooking. This very simple pasta came about one night when I really did not feel like going to the store but had to get dinner on the table for him. He loved it and so did I. It is now one of our favorite summer dishes.

Kosher salt
6 to 8 ounces dry pappardelle
2 tablespoons butter
2 or 3 garlic cloves, pressed
2 or 3 medium ripe tomatoes, peeled, seeded, and chopped
1 to 2 tablespoons crème fraîche or heavy cream
2 tablespoons chopped fresh Italian parsley, chives, or basil

Fill a large pot two-thirds full with water, season generously with salt, and bring to a boil over high heat. When the water reaches a rolling boil, add the pasta and stir gently until the water returns to a boil. Cook according to package directions until just done; stir now and then as it cooks. Drain but do not rinse the pasta.

Working quickly, put the butter into a medium sauté pan set over medium heat and, when it is melted, add the garlic and sauté for 30 seconds. Season with a little salt. Add the tomatoes and simmer very gently until they fall apart, about 4 to 5 minutes.

Stir in the crème fraîche or heavy cream, heat through, taste, correct for salt, and remove from the heat. Stir in the herbs and keep hot.

Tip the drained pasta into a wide bowl, add the sauce, and use two forks to lift the pasta several times to coat it with the sauce.

Divide between pasta bowls and serve immediately.

A Tomato Cookbook

Fresh Tomato Pasta
with Butter & Basil

Serves 3 or 4 as a main course, or 6 as a first course

You do not need a pasta machine to make homemade pasta, but if you do have one, by all means use it. The instructions here are for those who don't have such an appliance. Although this fresh pasta can be cut into any shape—ravioli, lasagne, tortellini, and so on—I prefer it as pappardelle or fettuccine.

1⅔ cups all-purpose flour
2 whole farm eggs
1 tablespoon double-concentrated tomato paste
Kosher salt
3 to 4 tablespoons best-quality butter, at room temperature
¾ cup freshly grated Parmigiano-Reggiano, Dry Jack, or similar cheese
¼ cup very thinly sliced fresh basil

Put the flour, 1 egg, and the tomato purée in a food processor and pulse until the mixture is well combined. Add the second egg and pulse again until the dough is uniformly moist and crumbly. Turn the dough out onto a floured work surface, gather it together, and knead it for 7 to 10 minutes, until it is as smooth as velvet. Cover with a tea towel and let rest for 45 minutes.

To begin rolling out the dough, which will be very stiff, flatten it by pressing it firmly with a rolling pin until it forms a circle. (If your work surface is particularly small, cut the dough in half and roll it out in two batches; it becomes quite large as it stretches.) Press and roll firmly and evenly until the dough is paper thin, about 5 to 10 minutes depending on your strength. Hang the strip of pasta dough on a drying rack over the edge of your cutting board or over a broom handle and let it air-dry for about 10 minutes. Return the sheet of dough to your work surface and sprinkle it lightly with flour.

To make pappardelle, roll up the dough lengthwise and, using a very sharp knife, cut through the roll at ½-inch intervals. To make fettuccine, cut it at ¼-inch intervals.

At this point, you will have pasta pinwheels that you must unravel carefully. Sprinkle them with a bit of flour or fine cornmeal and let them rest, covered with a towel, for up to an hour.

Put the butter into a wide, shallow bowl.

Fill a large pot half full with water, season generously with salt, and bring to a boil over high heat. When the water reaches a rolling boil, add the pasta and stir very gently. Cook for 1½ to 2 minutes and drain it thoroughly. Do not rinse it.

Working quickly, tip the pasta into the bowl with the butter, sprinkle the cheese on top, and use two forks to lift the pasta several times to coat it thoroughly as the butter melts. Season with salt and pepper and divide among individual pasta bowls or plates. Sprinkle basil on top and serve immediately.

Variation:
- Instead of butter and cheese, serve the pasta with either Tomato Butter (page 250) or Dried-Tomato Cream Sauce (page 279).

Linguine
with Sautéed Tomatoes, Chèvre & Fresh Herbs

Serves 3 to 4

Here is a simple dish for a busy weeknight when you don't have a lot of time to cook. The sauce pretty much makes itself once all of the ingredients are in the bowl.

12 ounces dried linguine
4 tablespoons extra-virgin olive oil
3 garlic cloves, peeled
3 cups cherry tomatoes, cut in half, or 4 medium slicing tomatoes, cut in wedges
Kosher salt
½ cup homemade chicken stock
4 ounces young chèvre
Black pepper in a mill
½ cup minced fresh herbs (basil, thyme, oregano, marjoram, Italian parsley, summer savory, chives)

Fill a large pot two-thirds full with water, season generously with salt, and bring to a boil over high heat. When the water reaches a rolling boil, add the pasta and stir until the water returns to a boil. Adjust the heat so that the water does not boil over and cook the pasta, stirring now and then, according to package directions until just done.

Meanwhile, warm about 2 tablespoons of olive oil in a heavy skillet, add the garlic, and sauté until it just begins to color. Remove and discard the garlic. Add the tomatoes and sauté quickly, agitating the pan so that they cook evenly. If using sliced tomatoes, turn the wedges once.

Transfer the tomatoes to a warm serving bowl and season lightly with salt. Add the chicken stock to the skillet, swirl to pick up any pan juices, and reduce by one-third.

Drain the pasta, do not rinse it, and tip it into the bowl with the sauce. Working quickly, break the chèvre over the pasta, add the herbs, and pour the chicken stock over all. Add the remaining olive oil, toss quickly and gently with two forks, correct for salt, season with black pepper, and serve immediately.

A Tomato Cookbook

Linguine
with Tomatoes, Oranges, Fennel, Currants & Olives

Serves 3 to 4

The flavors in this pasta sauce are evocative of Sicily, where fennel, all manner of citrus, and currants thrive. If you like sweet, salty, and savory flavors together, you should love this dish.

¼ cup currants
½ cup freshly squeezed orange juice
1 tablespoon olive oil
1 fennel bulb, trimmed and cut into
    small dice
Kosher salt
8 to 12 ounces dried linguine
Juice of ½ lemon
1 cup Tomato Concassé (page 263)
2 cloves garlic, crushed and minced
1 teaspoon minced ginger

2 tablespoons snipped chives
⅔ cup olives, pitted (oil-cured, salt-
    cured, brined) and chopped
1 orange, peeled, cut into sections,
    membranes removed
½ cup extra-virgin olive oil
Black pepper in a mill
½ cup pine nuts, lightly toasted
4 large radicchio leaves
3 radicchio leaves, shredded

Put the currants into a small bowl, add the orange juice and lemon juice, and set aside for 30 minutes.

Pour the olive oil into a small sauté pan set over medium heat, add the diced fennel, and sauté, turning frequently, until softened, about 7 to 8 minutes. Season with salt and transfer to a medium serving bowl.

Add the Tomato Concassé, garlic, ginger, chives, olives, and orange sections to the bowl with the fennel and toss together gently. Add the olive oil and several very generous turns of black pepper. Cover and set aside for 1 hour.

Fill a large pot two-thirds full with water, season generously with salt, and bring to a boil over high heat. When the water reaches a rolling boil, add the pasta and stir until the water returns to a boil. Adjust the heat so that the water does not boil over and cook the pasta, stirring now and then, according to package directions until just done.

Add the currants and the juice to the sauce.

Working quickly, drain the pasta and do not rinse it.

Tip it into the bowl with the sauce, add half the pine nuts, and use two forks to lift the pasta over and over to combine it thoroughly with the sauce.

Set the large radicchio leaves in individual pasta bowls and spoon pasta and sauce on top.

Garnish with julienned leaves and the remaining pine nuts and serve immediately.

Tomato Pasta
with Chicken, Olives & Dried-Tomato Cream Sauce

Serves 3 to 4

Dried-tomato cream sauce adds a richness to this simple yet hearty pasta dish, perfect as a quick dinner when there's leftover chicken in the refrigerator.

Dried–Tomato Cream Sauce (page 279)
1 recipe Tomato Pasta (page 179) or 12 ounces imported dried fettuccine
½ cup pitted olives, sliced (Kalamata, Niçoise, or California black ripe)
12 ounces cooked chicken thigh meat, in strips, warmed
4 small sprigs fresh thyme

Prepare the sauce and make the pasta in advance.

To finish the dish, fill a large pot two-thirds full with water, season generously with salt, and bring to a boil over high heat. When the water reaches a rolling boil, add the pasta and stir until the water returns to a boil. Adjust the heat so that the water does not boil over and cook the pasta, stirring now and then, according to directions until just done.

Pour the sauce into a small saucepan and warm over medium-low heat, and when it is hot transfer it to a serving bowl or mixing bowl.

When the pasta is done, drain it, do not rinse it, and add it to the sauce. Add the olives and chicken and use two forks to lift the pasta over and over until it is well coated. Turn gently to distributed the meat and olives.

Garnish with thyme sprigs and serve immediately.

Macaroni & Cheese
with Tomatoes & Pancetta

Serves 6 to 8

The best macaroni and cheese is rich, custardy, and voluptuous. Here, tomatoes add a tangy element. In the summer and early fall, use fresh tomatoes. Other times, use a good brand of canned tomatoes, and be sure to drain the liquid and reserve it for another use.

Kosher salt
1 pound ditalini
1 tablespoon olive oil
4 ounces pancetta, diced
4 farm eggs
3 cups heavy cream
2 cups diced tomatoes, drained
Black pepper in a mill
1 pound Italian Fontina, shredded
8 ounces Taleggio, in small chunks
½ cup chopped fresh Italian parsley
1½ cups fresh bread crumbs, toasted
Tabasco sauce

Preheat the oven to 350°F.

Fill a large pot two-thirds full with water, add 2 tablespoons of kosher salt, and bring to a boil over high heat. When the water reaches a rolling boil, add the pasta, stir until the water returns to a boil, and cook according to package directions until almost but not quite done. Stir now and then so that the pasta does not stick together. Drain, rinse, drain again, and set aside.

Meanwhile, heat the olive oil in a heavy skillet set over medium heat, add the pancetta, and fry until it loses its raw look but is not yet crisp. Set aside.

Break the eggs into a large mixing bowl and whisk until pale and smooth. Add the cream and tomatoes and whisk thoroughly. Season generously with black pepper. Fold in the cheeses and the drained pasta, add the pancetta and Italian parsley, taste, and correct for salt and pepper. Add several generous shakes of Tabasco sauce, if using, and pour the mixture into a large (4-quart) baking dish that has been coated with butter or olive oil.

Spread the bread crumbs on the top, cover tightly with aluminum foil, and bake for 30 minutes, removing the foil for the last 10 minutes.

Let rest for 5 minutes before serving.

Pappardelle
with Lamb Ragù

Serves 4 to 6

A traditional ragù, sometimes called Bolognese, is made with beef and is one of the classic Italian sauces. It is rich and voluptuous, with layers of flavor and a very small amount of tomato. Yet in America, many of us think of ragù as a tomato sauce, as commercial marinara sauces are often identified with the term. In the chapter on sauces, I offer a more traditional version than the one here, which I developed to pair with a specific Zinfandel from Dry Creek Valley.

2 pounds lamb shoulder or leg steak,
    cut into ¼-inch dice
Kosher salt
Black pepper in a mill
2 tablespoons butter
2 tablespoons olive oil
4 ounces pancetta, cut into ¼-inch
    dice
1 yellow onion, minced
2 carrots, peeled and cut into ⅛-inch
    dice
2 celery stalks, cut into ⅛-inch dice
1½ cups dry white wine

3 tablespoons double-concentrated
    tomato paste
2 teaspoons unsweetened cocoa
½ teaspoon ground cinnamon
3 cups duck, beef, or chicken stock
1 thyme sprig
2 parsley sprigs
1 cup half-and-half
1 pound dried pappardelle, bucatini,
    or fusilli col buco (long fusilli)
½ cup heavy cream or crème fraîche
1 medium chunk of Parmigiano-
    Reggiano or Vella Dry Jack.

Set a heavy pot—cast iron is ideal—over medium heat, add the lamb, and cook without stirring for 2 to 3 minutes. Stir and continue to cook until the meat is lightly browned. Season with salt and pepper, cook 2 minutes more, and transfer to a plate or bowl.

Return the pot to the heat, add the butter and olive oil, and, when the butter is melted, add the pancetta. Cook, stirring now and then, for 5 minutes, until the pancetta loses its raw look. Reduce the heat to low, add the onion, carrot, and celery, and sauté until very soft and fragrant, about 15 to 17 minutes.

Do not let the vegetables brown.

Season with salt and return the lamb and all its drippings to the pot.

Increase the heat to high, add the wine, and cook until it is nearly completely reduced. Lower the heat, stir in the tomato paste, cocoa, and cinnamon, add the stock, thyme sprig, and parsley sprigs.

Simmer very slowly for about 3½ hours, until the meat is very tender and the liquid nearly completely reduced. As the ragù cooks, stir in a splash of half-and-half every now and then.

When the meat is completely tender, cover the pan, remove from the heat, and let rest about 30 minutes.

Uncover and use a wide spoon to scoop off and discard the fat that collects on the surface of the ragù. Use tongs to remove and discard the herb sprigs.

While the ragù rests, fill a large pot two-thirds full with water, season generously with salt, and bring to a rolling boil over high heat. Add the pasta, stir until the water returns to a boil, adjust the heat, and cook the pasta according to package directions until just done. Drain and do not rinse. Put the pasta into a wide, shallow bowl and keep hot.

Working quickly, pour the cream or crème fraîche into a small saucepan, set over medium-low heat, stir, and heat through.

Return the ragù to medium heat, stir in the hot cream or crème fraîche, and heat through. Taste and correct for salt and pepper.

Spoon half the ragù onto the pasta and use two forks to gently lift the pasta in several places to distribute the ragù. Spoon the remaining ragù over the pasta, grate cheese over the top, and serve immediately, with the remaining cheese and a grater alongside.

> **Variation:**
> Serve the ragù over creamy polenta instead of pasta.

Tomato & Polenta Tart
with Basil Mayonnaise

Serves 4 to 6

I could eat this tart every day during tomato season. It is wonderful straight from the oven with freshly picked salad greens on the side, and equally delicious the next day cold, right out of the refrigerator. It also reheats quite well.

½ cup coarse–ground polenta, preferably organic
2 tablespoons butter
2 teaspoons kosher salt, plus more for seasoning
¼ cup all-purpose flour
3 medium ripe tomatoes, peeled, cored, and cut into thin rounds
Black pepper in a mill
4 ounces (1 cup) grated Dry Jack or other similar cheese
1 cup basil leaves, loosely packed
Juice of ½ lemon
¾ cup homemade or best-quality mayonnaise

Set a 10- to 12-inch tart pan next to your work surface.

Pour 2½ cups of water into a heavy saucepan, whisk in the polenta, set over medium heat, and bring to a boil, stirring constantly. Reduce the heat so that the polenta simmers gently. Stir it continuously until it thickens and then stir it frequently.

After the polenta is quite thick—in about 10 minutes—add the butter, stir, and add the 2 teaspoons of salt and the flour. Stir continuously until the mixture is very thick and begins to pull away from the sides of the pan.

Working quickly, rinse the inside of the tart pan with water and do not dry it.

Pour the polenta into the pan and use a rubber spatula to spread it evenly. Press the tomatoes into the polenta, overlapping them slightly. Cover and set aside so that the polenta sets up.

A Tomato Cookbook

Preheat the oven to 325°F.

When the polenta is fairly firm, season the tomatoes with salt and pepper and spread the cheese over them.

Set on the middle rack of the oven and cook for about 15 minutes, until the cheese has taken on some color.

Meanwhile, chop the basil and transfer it to a small bowl. Season with salt, add the lemon juice, and fold in the mayonnaise. Taste and correct for salt and acid.

Remove the tart from the oven, let rest for 15 minutes, drizzle basil mayonnaise over it, cut into wedges, and serve, with the remaining basil mayonnaise alongside.

Meyer Lemon Risotto
with Tomato Concassé

Serves 3 to 4

Creamy risotto makes a wonderful main course but is also delicious when served as a bed for sautéed fish such as snapper and Petrale sole, seared scallops, braised beef, or braised lamb shanks. This one, with its tangy burst of lemon, is perfect with almost any seafood. For a simpler risotto and for times when lemons are not available, omit the lemon zest, juice, and segments.

1¼ cups Tomato Concassé (page 263)
1 garlic clove, pressed
Zest of 1 Meyer lemon
5 tablespoons fresh Meyer lemon juice
Kosher salt
Black pepper in a mill
6 cups homemade chicken broth or
    2 cups homemade chicken stock
    combined with 4 cups water, hot
2 tablespoons butter
1 small white onion, diced

1 shallot, minced
1¼ cups Vialone Nano rice
4 ounces triple cream cheese (such
    as Brillat–Savarin or L'Aviatur),
    or best–quality Brie (such as
    Chantal Plaas Raw Milk Brie or
    Brie de Meaux)
1 Meyer lemon, peeled and seeded,
    with membranes removed
2 tablespoons minced fresh Italian
    parsley

Make the Tomato Concassé, add the garlic, half the lemon zest, and 1 tablespoon of the lemon juice. Stir, taste, and season with salt and pepper.

Keep the chicken broth or stock in a saucepan set over medium-low heat. Heat the butter in a medium-sized pan set over medium heat. Add the onion and sauté until it is soft and fragrant, about 8 minutes. Add the shallot and sauté for 4 minutes more. Season with salt and pepper. Add the rice and stir with a wooden spoon until each grain begins to turn milky white, about 2 minutes.

Add the stock a half cup at a time, stirring after each addition until the liquid is nearly absorbed. Continue to add stock and stir until the rice is tender, about 16 to 20 minutes total cooking time. When the rice is almost tender, stir in the remaining lemon zest, remaining lemon juice, and cheese. Taste, correct the seasoning, and stir in a final ¼ cup of stock. Remove from the heat, quickly fold in the lemon, and ladle into soup plates.

Spoon concassé over each portion, top with Italian parsley, and serve immediately.

Hot Rice
with Cool Tomatoes

Serves 2 to 4

One of my favorite cookbooks is Unplugged Kitchen *(Morrow, 1996) by Viana LaPlace, which is a beautiful study in grace, simplicity, and deliciousness. It is the only cookbook, other than my own and the 1964 edition of* Joy of Cooking, *that I keep on a small shelf next to my iMac. Hot Rice with Cold Lemon is one of my favorite recipes in the book and this dish is inspired by that one. I often make it just for myself during late summer and early fall, when there is an abundance of dead-ripe tomatoes.*

⅔ cup Italian or Spanish rice
Kosher salt
1 large beefsteak tomato, cored and chopped
1 garlic clove, minced
½ lemon
Extra-virgin olive oil
Black pepper in a mill
Chopped fresh Italian parsley or snipped chives, optional

Put the rice into a medium saucepan, and add a few generous pinches of salt and enough water to cover it by a good 3 inches. Bring to a boil over high heat, reduce the heat to medium, and cook until the rice is just done but still with some resistance at its center; it will take about 12 to 14 minutes.

While the rice cooks, put the chopped tomato into a bowl, add the garlic and lemon juice, season to taste with salt, and set aside.

When the rice is ready, drain it and divide among soup plates or pasta bowls. Top with the tomato and its juices, drizzle with olive oil, season with several generous turns of black pepper, and scatter with herbs, if using. Enjoy immediately.

Eggs

Eggs are one of the foods that have gotten so much better in the last decade or so. Farm eggs have always been good but they haven't been as readily available as they are now for decades. Today, even people who live in the city may keep a few laying hens, and great eggs are available at farmers markets and farm stands if you can't have your own. Some so-called experts claim that there is no difference in taste between factory-farm eggs and eggs from small flocks of pastured chickens, that the only reason to pay the substantially higher price is because we know it is the right thing to do. Certainly, pastured chickens live a much happier life than their confined cousins. But the difference in tastes is staggering. Once you've had a great farm egg it is nearly impossible to be satisfied with cheap eggs from supermarkets. The recipes in this section highlight my favorite ways of enjoying farm eggs and summer tomatoes together.

Avocado Omelet with Warm Cherry Tomato Vinaigrette
Souffléd Omelet with Variations
Eggs Poached in Tomato Sauce
Shakshouka
Green Shakshouka

Avocado Omelet
with Warm Cherry Tomato Vinaigrette

Serves 2

When you have great eggs, humble dishes such as omelets blossom. An omelet such as this one makes as satisfying a dinner as it does a breakfast.

Warm Cherry Tomato Vinaigrette (page 280)
½ firm-ripe Hass avocado
4 large farm eggs
Kosher salt
Black pepper in a mill
4 teaspoons butter

Make the vinaigrette, set it aside, and keep warm.

Cut the avocado into very thin lengthwise slices, use a large spoon to scoop out the flesh, and set it aside briefly.

Break 2 eggs into two small bowls, add 2 teaspoons of warm water to both bowls, and beat the eggs until smooth. Season with salt and pepper.

Set a 9-inch omelet pan over high heat, add half the butter, and when it is very foamy, tip the pan to coat it fully. Working quickly, tip in 2 eggs and let cook, without stirring, for about 90 seconds. Continue to cook while using a fork to whip the unset eggs into tender curds, being certain not to reach down through the set portion. When the eggs are fully cooked but still moist, spread half the avocado slices over half the omelet (the half on the opposite side of the handle). Use a spatula to lift the portion of the omelet near the handle over the avocado and tip the omelet onto a plate.

Repeat with the second dish of eggs.

Spoon warm tomato vinaigrette over the omelets and serve immediately.

Souffléd Omelet

with Variations

Serves 3 to 4

A souffled omelet, sometimes called a puffed or puffy omelet, takes a bit more time than other types of omelets, but it is easy to make and has a lovely ethereal quality, like a spring cloud. Serve it for breakfast with roasted potatoes and for dinner with a big green salad or platter of sliced summer tomatoes.

6 large pastured eggs, separated into large bowls
1 tablespoon butter, cut into small cubes
Kosher salt
Black pepper in a mill
¼ cup cold water
2 tablespoons butter
½ cup Tomato Coulis, Red or Golden (pages 264 and 264), hot

Preheat the oven to 350°F.

Whisk the egg yolks until pale and smooth, add the butter cubes, a generous few pinches of salt, and several generous turns of black pepper, and whisk together thoroughly. Set aside briefly.

Whisk or beat the egg whites until they are quite foamy. Add the cold water and continue to whisk until the eggs form soft peaks that hold their shape when the mixer or whisk is lifted. Use a rubber spatula to gently fold the yolk mixture into the whites, being sure not to overmix, as you don't want to lose the egg white's loft.

Put the 2 tablespoons of butter into a heavy pan, preferably one with sloping sides, such as an All-Clad Saucier. Alternately, use a cast-iron frying pan. Set over medium-high heat and when the butter is melted, tip the pan to coat the sides with the butter.

Pour the egg mixture into the pan and, without stirring, cook for 3 to 4 minutes, until the bottom and sides are set. Transfer to the oven and cook until the omelet is puffed, the middle set, and the top lightly browned, about 12 minutes or a bit longer.

Remove from the oven and use a rubber spatula to loosen the sides. Cut the omelet into wedges and transfer to individual plates. Spoon sauce over each portion and serve immediately.

Variations:

- Omit the Tomato Coulis and serve with a dollop of tomato-onion relish and a dollop of crème fraîche.

- Scatter about 3 ounces of crumbled feta cheese over the cooked omelet, top with quartered cherry tomatoes, cut into wedges, and serve.

Eggs Poached in Tomato Sauce

Serves 4

Eggs served, and often cooked, in tomato sauce are a tradition around the world, or nearly so. Italian Uova in Purgatorio and Mexican Huevos Rancheros are two of the most familiar versions in America. This version, which uses vinegar to accent the tomato's flavor, is wonderful served atop thick slices of grilled or toasted country-style bread. It is also delightful served over grilled polenta.

2 tablespoons pure olive oil
1 small red onion, peeled and diced
1 cup chicken stock
2 cups tomato sauce, fresh, home-canned, or commercial
¼ teaspoon crushed red pepper
2 tablespoons red wine vinegar
Kosher salt
Black pepper in a mill
4 large farm eggs
4 thick slices of country-style hearth bread
2 cloves of garlic, cut in half
1 tablespoon chopped fresh Italian parsley

Heat the olive oil in a large, heavy sauté pan set over low heat, add the onion, and sauté until soft and very fragrant, about 15 to 20 minutes. Add the chicken stock, increase the heat to medium, and simmer until reduced by half. Stir in the tomato sauce, lower the heat, and simmer for 30 minutes.

Stir in the crushed red pepper and the vinegar and season to taste with salt and several turns of pepper.

Carefully break an egg into a small bowl and slip it into the sauce; continue until all eggs are added. Spoon a little sauce over the eggs and cook until the whites are set and the yolks still liquid, about 4 to 5 minutes.

Working quickly, toast the bread lightly, rub each slice with a cut clove of garlic, and set in individual plates. Using a large spoon, set an egg on top of each piece of bread. Divide the sauce among the portions, sprinkle with parsley and several turns of black pepper, and serve immediately.

Shakshouka
Eggs Baked in Spicy Tomato Sauce

Serves 1

Shakshouka is popular throughout the Middle East and for good reason: it is extraordinarily delicious. You find similar versions in other parts of the Mediterranean, all the way to Spain, where it is common to find sliced chorizo in the sauce. It is typically prepared in a clay pot, often a large one that serves several people. In this version, I make a single serving, a perfect dinner on a cool fall night. It is easily doubled or tripled and you can make it in either individual pots or one large one. Just make sure the sauce is good—this means tasting it several times as you prepare it—and do not overcook the eggs; the yolks should be hot but still liquid.

2 tablespoons olive oil
½ small yellow onion, cut into small dice
3 to 4 garlic cloves, minced
Kosher salt
1 to 2 teaspoons hot Spanish paprika, to taste
1 to 2 teaspoons smoked Spanish paprika, to taste
¾ teaspoon ground cumin
2 to 3 medium ripe tomatoes, cored and peeled
1 to 2 Anaheim-type chilies or 1 poblano, seared, peeled, seeded, and cut
    into medium julienne
2 farm eggs, at room temperature
2 ounces feta cheese, broken into pieces
2 tablespoons chopped fresh Italian parsley or cilantro
Black pepper in a mill
Hot hearth bread or lightly toasted pita

Put the olive oil into a small sauté pan set over medium heat, add the onion, and sauté until soft and fragrant, about 8 to 10 minutes. Add the garlic, sauté 2 minutes more, season with salt, and stir in the paprikas and cumin.

Hold a peeled tomato in your dominant hand and crush it into the pan; do the same with the other tomato. Stir in the chilies, taste, and correct for salt and pepper.

At this point, I prefer to tip the sauce into the clay pot known as a bram, a small one that has been warmed. I then put it into a toaster oven, set the temperature at 300°F, and then raise it incrementally until it reaches 400°F (the slow heating protects the bram). (If you don't have a bram, use another type of small clay or porcelain dish, or poach the eggs in the sauce on top of the stove.)

When the sauce is bubbling hot, break one of the eggs into a small bowl, gently tip it into the bram, do the same with the second egg, and return it to the oven. When the egg whites seem almost done, set the oven to "broil" and cook 2 minutes more.

Carefully remove the bram, set it on a small wooden cutting board, scatter with feta and either parsley or cilantro, season with several turns of black pepper, and enjoy immediately, with hot bread alongside.

Variation:
- To serve with sausage, fry a Spanish-style chorizo or a Moroccan merguez until just done; cool slightly, cut into thin rounds, and add to the sauce before adding the eggs.

Green Shakshouka

Serves 2 to 3

As I was working on this book, I had to make a quick trip to New York City, where I stayed on Lafayette Street in Soho. A sweet little restaurant, Jack's Wife Freda, was a short walk from my hotel and I stopped there on my first morning for breakfast. When I saw Green Shakshouka on their menu, I did a mental cartwheel and ordered it instantly. It was as delicious as I had hoped and I went back the next day to enjoy it again. This is roughly their version, which proprietor Maya Jankelowitz shared with me, along with a couple of my own flourishes, the serranos because I love their flavor and the cilantro for the same reason.

1 pint (8 to 10 ounces) green tomatillos, husks removed, washed, halved
1 small onion, chopped
3 garlic cloves, crushed
2 large poblanos, seared, peeled, stemmed, seeded, and chopped
1 or 2 serranos, peeled, seared, stemmed, seeded, and chopped
¾ cup fresh Italian parsley leaves, chopped
½ to 1 teaspoon cumin
½ cup fresh cilantro leaves, chopped
Kosher salt
4 to 6 large farm eggs
Hot hearth bread or toasted brioche

Set a dry cast-iron or other heavy skillet over high heat, add the tomatoes, onion, and garlic, and cook, turning frequently, until the tomatillos have softened and the onion has picked up a bit of color.

Let cool and tip into the work bowl of a food processor fitted with its metal blade and pulse until smooth. Pass the mixture through a strainer to remove the tomatillo seeds, return the purée to the work bowl, and add the poblanos, serranos, parsley, half the cilantro, and the cumin, and season with salt. Pulse several times, until nearly smooth.

Return to the skillet, correct for salt, and warm over high heat. Stir in the remaining cilantro.

Preheat the oven to 350°F.

Break the eggs, one at a time, into 6-inch round porcelain ramekins or similar ovenproof containers, putting 2 eggs into each dish. Spoon sauce over the eggs, filling the container nearly full. Bake for 8 to 10 minutes, or a bit longer, until the egg whites are set and the yolks still liquid.

Transfer each ramekin to a heavy plate or small wooden cutting board, season with a little salt, and serve with bread or broiche.

Vegetable Dishes

Tomatoes are much more common as a side dish, as an accompaniment to other foods, than they are as a main dish, where you typically find them as a supporting player rather than the star. As sides, they soar, both as themselves and in the way they combine with other flavors on the plate. When I was a little girl, my favorite sickbed food, enjoyed when I was finally on the mend, was a rare steak with diced fresh tomatoes; it was so good that I'd drink the juices that mingled in the center of the plate, a combination I still love. The recipes in this chapter celebrate summer and fall tomatoes, when it is abundance that most inspires us.

Grilled Cherry Tomatoes
Baked Cherry Tomatoes with Four Variations
Tomatoes Provençal
Fried Tomatoes with Herbs & Cream
Tomato Gratin with Fresh Basil
Fried Green Tomatoes with Cream, Bacon & Cilantro
Stuffed Tomatoes with Four Variations
Green Beans and Potatoes with Warm Cherry Tomato Vinaigrette
Grilled Cabbage with Warm Cherry Tomato Vinaigrette

Grilled Cherry Tomatoes

Serves 6

These grilled tomatoes are so easy to make, so beautiful, and so delicious that they should be part of every summer barbecue. If you are pressed for time, they are an easy and impressive dish to take to a potluck, too, provided there will be a grill.

1 dozen 12-inch wooden skewers, soaked in water for 30 minutes
4 dozen firm-ripe cherry tomatoes, preferably a mix of colors
2 small red onions, cut into wedges
Salad mix, arugula, or 1 bunch parsley
Kosher salt and freshly ground black pepper

Start a fire in a charcoal grill or heat a stovetop grill. Thread 4 tomatoes onto each of the 12 skewers, alternating with a single piece of onion.

When the coals are hot, set the skewers on a grill rack and turn every 2 minutes until the tomatoes begin to crack and sizzle.

Spread the salad mix, arugula, or parsley over a platter, set the skewers of tomatoes on top, season with salt and pepper, and serve hot.

Baked Cherry Tomatoes
with Four Variations

Serves 4 to 6

If you have a garden, you likely have a hard time keeping up with cherry tomatoes at the height of their season. This dish will help. It takes minutes to prepare and is good hot, warm, or chilled. Enjoy it as a side dish, spoon it over rice, quinoa, or creamy polenta, toss it with pasta, and serve it with toasted hearth bread. These tomatoes are also delicious served over a grilled skirt steak sandwich.

1 quart cherry tomatoes
5 or 6 garlic cloves, peeled and sliced
2 tablespoons snipped chives or chopped fresh Italian parsley
¼ cup extra-virgin olive oil
Juice of 1 lemon
Kosher salt
Black pepper in a mill

Preheat the oven to 350°F.

Put the tomatoes into a baking dish, add the garlic and chives, and toss. Pour the olive oil and lemon juice over the tomatoes, season with salt and pepper, and set on the middle rack of the oven. Cook for 20 to 30 minutes, until the tomatoes have burst open.

Remove from the oven. Serve hot or let cool, chill, and serve cold.

Variations:
- With pesto: Before serving hot, top with 2 or 3 tablespoons of homemade pesto.

- With Chimichurri: Before serving hot, top with 2 or 3 tablespoons of Chimichurri, (page 251); this is ideal when serving the tomatoes with beef, especially grilled rare steak.

A Tomato Cookbook

- With chèvre and tapenade: Set a log of chèvre on a wide, shallow serving bowl and spoon the tomatoes and their juices over it. Top with a generous dollop or two of tapenade. To make a simple tapenade, combine ½ cup pitted and minced Niçoise or Kalamata olives, 3 minced garlic cloves, 2 mashed anchovy fillets, 1 tablespoon minced fresh Italian parsley, and ⅓ cup extra-virgin olive oil.

- With anchovies: Put 4 or 5 anchovy fillets in a small bowl and add 3 tablespoons of red wine vinegar. Let sit 30 minutes and then add to the tomatoes before cooking them. Omit the lemon juice.

Tomatoes Provençal

Serves 6

Serve this classic dish alongside roasted chicken, grilled rib eye steak, creamy polenta, or risotto or set atop a small bed of fresh salad greens and serve as a first course or light lunch. Many versions simply cut tomatoes in half but I prefer this method.

6 medium firm-ripe tomatoes
4 cloves garlic, thinly sliced
4 tablespoons extra-virgin olive oil
Kosher salt
Black pepper in a mill
1 cup fresh bread crumbs
2 garlic cloves, crushed and minced
2 tablespoons finely minced fresh Italian parsley

Preheat the oven to 375°F.

Cut a slice off the stem ends of the tomatoes just above the shoulder (where the tomato begins to widen). Carefully pierce the tomatoes several times with a fork, pointing the tines down directly into the flesh but being careful not to puncture the skin. Set them in a baking dish and top each with several slices of garlic, pressing the slices down into the flesh of the tomatoes. Drizzle with a little olive oil and add a pinch of salt and a turn of black pepper.

Put the bread crumbs into a small bowl, season with salt and pepper, add the minced garlic and parsley, and pour in the remaining olive oil. Toss with a fork. Spoon on top of the tomatoes.

Set on the middle rack of the oven and cook until the tomatoes are soft and the topping is lightly browned, about 25 to 35 minutes, or a bit longer, depending on the variety of tomato.

Remove from the oven, let rest 5 minutes, and serve hot.

Fried Tomatoes
with Herbs & Cream

Serves 4 to 6

Work fast and carefully to make these sensational tomatoes so that they hold their shape; if you linger, cook at too low a heat, or agitate the tomatoes too much, they will turn themselves into sauce. Serve with hot bread alongside.

4 large firm–ripe tomatoes, cored
2 tablespoons snipped chives
2 tablespoons minced fresh Italian
    parsley
2 tablespoons minced fresh cilantro
4 cloves garlic, peeled and minced
2 serranos, minced

2 tablespoons butter
½ cup dry white wine
½ cup heavy cream
Kosher salt and freshly ground black
    pepper
Herb sprigs, for garnish

Cut the tomatoes into ⅜-inch-thick slices, discarding the stem and blossom ends, and set them on a plate or glass baking dish, arranging them in a single layer. Sprinkle the herbs, garlic, and serrano over the tomatoes. Cover the tomatoes with a tea towel and let them rest for about 3 hours.

Put the butter into a large, heavy sauté pan set over medium-high heat, add the tomatoes in a single layer and cook for 2 minutes, turn, and cook for 2 minutes more. Work in batches so that you do not crowd the tomatoes. Set the cooked tomatoes on a serving platter and keep warm in a slow oven.

Increase the heat to high, add the wine, and swirl to deglaze the pan. When the wine is nearly completely reduced, tip any juices that have collected on the plates with the tomatoes into the pan, add the cream, and reduce by about one-third.

Taste the sauce, correct for salt and pepper, and pour over the tomatoes. Garnish with herb sprigs and serve hot.

Tomato Gratin
with Fresh Basil

Serves 4 to 6

Enjoy this dish in the fall, when the tomatoes are dead ripe and evenings have turned cool. It is rich, luscious, and deeply satisfying. Make it the centerpiece of the meal, with hot bread and a big green salad alongside or serve it as a side dish with fish, poultry, or beef.

6 medium ripe tomatoes, cored and cut into ⅜-inch-thick rounds
¾ cup heavy cream
1 basil sprig
Kosher salt
Black pepper in a mill
¾ cup fresh bread crumbs
8 to 10 basil leaves, cut into very thin slices

Preheat the oven to 425°F.

Arrange the tomatoes in a single layer in a shallow baking dish, overlapping them slightly so that they will fit. Season with salt and pepper and set aside.

Pour the cream into a small, heavy saucepan, add the sprig of basil, and reduce the cream by half over high heat, watching it closely so that it doesn't boil over. Remove from the heat and use tongs to remove and discard the basil sprig.

Spoon the cream over the tomatoes, season with a little salt and pepper, and scatter the bread crumbs on top.

Set on the middle rack of the oven, bake for 15 minutes or until the tomatoes are tender and juicy, and remove from the heat. Let rest for 5 minutes, scatter the basil on top, and serve.

Fried Green Tomatoes
with Cream, Bacon & Cilantro

Serves 4 to 6

Most fried green tomatoes are coated heavily with cornmeal, flour, or bread crumbs, and sometimes all three, and fried until very crisp on the outside. This version is both lighter and richer. Serve it with roasted pork shoulder, roasted chicken, or almost any kind of barbecue, including ribs.

3 slices of bacon, fried until crisp, drained
4 medium green (unripe) tomatoes
5-ounce log of chèvre, such as chabis
½ cup fine-ground cornmeal
Kosher salt and freshly ground pepper
½ cup heavy cream
¼ cup chopped fresh cilantro

Chop or crumble the bacon and set it aside.

Cut and discard the stems and blossom ends of the tomatoes and cut each tomato into ⅜-inch-thick slices. Let the sliced tomatoes rest on absorbent paper or a tea towel. Slice the goat cheese into thin rounds and set it aside.

Preheat the oven to 300°F.

Mix together the cornmeal, salt, and pepper and dredge each slice of tomato in the mixture. Drain off all but 4 tablespoons of bacon fat and fry the tomatoes in the remaining fat over medium heat until the cornmeal browns, about 1½ minutes on each side. After turning the tomato slices once, top each with a round of goat cheese and place the pan in the oven for 5 minutes.

Transfer the tomatoes to a warm plate, set the pan over medium heat, and add the cream. Swirl to pick up any pan drippings, and, when the cream is hot, pour it over the tomatoes.

Scatter the bacon and the cilantro over the tomatoes and serve hot.

Stuffed Tomatoes
with Four Variations

Serves 6

A medium tomato—slightly bigger than a tennis ball—with its insides scooped out makes the perfect edible serving dish. Cooks and chefs have been filling tomatoes with all manner of savory mixtures for decades. In the 1950s, tomatoes were typically filled with cottage cheese, tuna salad, deviled egg salad, and chicken salad, all of which remain somewhat common today, depending on where you live. Many of the salads in this book, such as Lakeville Tabbouleh (page 134), work beautifully when served in a tomato.

Basic technique:

Cut and discard the stem end of each tomato about a quarter inch down, just above its wide shoulder. Use a grapefruit spoon to cut out the seeds, gel, and most of the flesh, being careful not to cut through the skin. Set the tomatoes cut side down on absorbent toweling until ready to fill them. (Reserve the flesh and juice for another use.)

To fill:

Simply spoon the chosen filling into the cavity, adding enough so that it comes up a bit over the top of the tomato. If the stuffed tomatoes will be baked, set them on a baking dish brushed with a little olive oil. If they will be served raw, set them on a bed of greens on a serving platter or on individual plates and add appropriate garnish.

Allow about ⅓ cup of filling for each tomato.

Filling suggestions:

Seed-Shaped Pasta: Mix any seed-shaped pasta (acini di pepe, orzo, rosemarina, melone) with fresh minced herbs, extra-virgin olive oil, a little lemon juice or red wine vinegar, and crumbled feta cheese. Season to taste with kosher salt and black pepper. Fill the tomatoes and serve right away.

Bay Shrimp: Mix bay shrimp with minced red onion, snipped chives, mayonnaise, lemon juice, and several turns of black pepper. Add salt to taste. Fill the tomatoes with the mixture and serve right away.

Meyer Lemon Risotto: Make the risotto (page 193) and let it rest for about 30 minutes. Spoon the cooled risotto into the tomatoes, set in a baking dish, and cook in a 325°F oven for 20 to 25 minutes, until the risotto is hot and the tomatoes are cooked. Remove from the oven, set on individual plates, and spoon Tomato Concassé on top. Serve hot.

Polenta: This one takes a little more time, but the results are well worth it. Prepare 6 to 8 sturdy tomatoes for stuffing. Add ½ cup coarse-ground polenta and 1 teaspoon kosher salt to 2½ cups cold water in a heavy pot and set over medium heat. Stir continuously until the mixture comes to a boil, and then reduce the heat and simmer, stirring regularly, until the polenta thickens, about 15 to 25 minutes. Stir in 2 tablespoons of butter, 2 ounces (about ½ cup) of grated cheese, several turns of black pepper, and 2 tablespoons of chopped fresh Italian parsley. Continue cooking over low heat, and when the polenta pulls away from the side of the pan, remove it from the heat and let it cool for about 10 minutes. Use a soup spoon or small ladle to fill the tomatoes with the polenta. Set the filled tomatoes in a baking dish brushed with olive oil and bake in a 325°F oven for 20 to 25 minutes, until the tomatoes are cooked. Remove from the oven, dust each with some finely grated cheese, garnish with a sprig of Italian parsley, and serve hot.

Green Beans and Potatoes
with Warm Cherry Tomato Vinaigrette

Serves 3 to 4, easily doubled

If you are trying to eat or get your family to eat more vegetables, this is a great way to do it, as the flavors are irresistible and the dish goes with almost anything, from rice pilaf to roast beef. Leftovers make a great salad but be sure to remove from the refrigerator thirty minutes before serving.

Kosher salt
8 to 10 ounces small fingerling potatoes, washed
8 ounces small Blue Lake green beans, trimmed
Warm Cherry Tomato Vinaigrette (page 280), preferably with Sungold
   tomatoes
Black pepper in a mill
3 tablespoons chopped fresh Italian parsley, snipped chives, or fresh basil cut
   into thin slices

Fill a medium saucepan half full with water, add a generous tablespoon of salt, and bring to a boil over high heat.

If the potatoes are very small, cut them in half lengthwise; if they are big, cut them into lengthwise quarters. Add them to the water and when it reaches a rolling boil, reduce the heat to medium. Cook for 5 minutes and test for doneness. If they are nearly tender, add the green beans. If not, cook another few minutes, test again, and, if ready, add the green beans.

Cook for 5 minutes more.

While the vegetables cook, make the vinaigrette.

Drain the vegetables, shaking off excess water, and tip them into a wide, shallow serving bowl. Pour the vinaigrette over them, season with several turns of black pepper and a light sprinkling of salt, add the parsley, and serve hot or warm.

Grilled Cabbage
with Warm Cherry Tomato Vinaigrette

Serves 4 to 6

When cabbage is grilled, its sweetness blossoms, which in turn goes beautifully with a tangy tomato vinaigrette. These wedges retain a good bit of their characteristic crunch. If you prefer your cabbage more fully cooked, wait until the coals are just beginning to cool down a bit and set the cabbage on the perimeter of the grill rack, so that it is not directly above the coals.

1 small firm green cabbage, cored and cut into wedges
Warm Cherry Tomato Vinaigrette (page 280)
4 bacon slices, fried until crisp, drained and crumbled, optional

Prepare a fire in a charcoal grill or heat a stovetop grill. When the fire is hot, set the cabbage on a clean grill rack and cook for about 4 minutes; turn and cook 4 minutes more or a bit longer.

Transfer the cabbage wedges to a platter, spoon vinaigrette on top, and scatter the bacon on everything, if using.

Serve hot.

Flesh
Fish, Shellfish, Poultry & Meat

When it comes to the main courses, tomatoes rarely take center stage. A tomato is a supporting player, an important one and even a crucial one, but rarely stands on its own for a monologue or solo performance.

When it comes to seafood, tomatoes have a long, delicious history with both fish and shellfish. From shrimp and crab cocktails—one or the other napped in a mildly spicy tomato-based cocktail sauce—to slow-cooked stews, braises, and tagines from around the world, tomatoes are used to add both flavor and acidity to nearly every type of seafood.

Some of the simplest preparations are the most wonderful: sautéed snapper folded into a soft corn tortilla and topped with fresh tomato salsa; warm tomato vinaigrette spooned over pan-fried Petrale sole; oysters on the half shell with a delicate tomato mignonette. All are so good and so easy to prepare at home.

When it comes to poultry and meats, there are many classic preparations, including one of my favorites, chicken cacciatore, which I offer here using summer tomatoes, and Boeuf Bourguignonne, one of France's greatest contributions to world cuisine.

Picado
Shrimp with Tomato Essence, Olive Oil & Basil
Mussels with Tomatoes, Garlic, Chorizo & White Wine
San Francisco–Style Cioppino
Rosefish Veracruz
Tomato Halibut Tagine
Summer Chicken Cacciatore
Ficandó
Boeuf Bourguignonne
Beef, Cherry Tomatoes & Mushrooms on Skewers
Provençal-Style Leg of Lamb with Onions, Potatoes, Tomatoes & Rosemary

Picado

Makes about ⅓ cup

2 garlic cloves, peeled and crushed
Pinch of salt
¼ cup hazelnuts, toasted and peeled
¼ cup almonds, toasted and peeled

Put the crushed garlic in a mortar or other hand grinder, add a generous pinch of salt, and crush the garlic to a paste. Add the nuts and use the pestle to crush each one. After the nuts are crushed, continue to grind the mixture until it forms a nearly smooth, uniform paste. Set aside until ready to use.

Shrimp
with Tomato Essence, Olive Oil & Basil

Serves 2 to 4

I love this dish when I can get Gulf shrimp or other wild shrimp. It is at once robust and delicate, perfect on a hot summer night. To serve as a first course, peel the shrimp, arrange them on individual plates, and spoon the tomato essence on top.

1 pound large Gulf shrimp or other medium to large wild shrimp, cleaned, shells on
Kosher salt
Black pepper in a mill
1 teaspoon hot Spanish paprika, plus more to taste
3 tablespoons butter
1 tablespoon Rainwater Madeira or dry sherry
⅔ cup Tomato Essence (page 267)
¼ cup good-quality extra-virgin olive oil
¼ cup fresh basil leaves, loosely packed, cut into very thin strips

Set the shrimp on a clean work surface and season all over with salt, pepper, and paprika.

Melt the butter in a heavy skillet, set over medium-high heat, and, when it is fully melted, add the garlic, sauté 1 minute, add the shrimp, and sauté for about 1 to 2 minutes, until they just begin to lose their raw color. Turn and cook 1 to 2 minutes more. Remove from the heat and tip into a medium serving bowl.

Working quickly, return the pan to the heat, add the Madeira or sherry, swirl the pan to pick up any juices, and pour over the shrimp.

Add the Tomato Essence, olive oil, and basil and agitate the bowl gently.

Serve immediately and enjoy with your fingers, with hot bread to sop up the delicious juices.

Mussels

with Tomatoes, Garlic, Chorizo & White Wine

Serves 3 to 4

Originally, I made this dish with bulk Mexican-style chorizo, as Spanish chorizo was very hard to find. Now that it is widely available, I use Spanish chorizo or any other artisan chorizo made by local producers. Do not use the Mexican chorizo that comes in plastic links.

1 pound Spanish-style fresh chorizo, skins pierced with a fork
2 shallots, minced
3 garlic cloves, minced
1 serrano, minced
Kosher salt
Black pepper in a mill
Pinch of crushed red pepper flakes
2 cups Tomato Concassé (page 263)
1 cup dry white wine
½ lemon
3 pounds PEI mussels, rinsed
2 tablespoons chopped fresh Italian parsley or cilantro
Hot hearth bread

Put the chorizo in a heavy medium saucepan set over medium heat and fry, turning frequently, until just cooked through. Use tongs to transfer to a plate.

Add the shallots, garlic, and serrano, reduce the heat to low, and cook until soft and fragrant, about 12 minutes. Do not let brown. Season with salt, several turns of black pepper, and a generous pinch of red pepper flakes.

Add the Tomato Concassé and the white wine and squeeze in the juice from the lemon.

Working quickly, cut the chorizo into thin half moons and add them to the pan.

Increase the heat to high, add the mussels, cover and agitate the pan gently and frequently, for 4 to 5 minutes, until the mussels open.

Remove from the heat and use tongs to remove any mussels that have not opened.

Use a large slotted spoon to divide the mussels among individual soup plates or pasta bowls. Divide the space over each portion, sprinkle with parsley or cilantro, and serve immediately, with plenty of hot bread alongside.

San Francisco–Style Cioppino

Serves 6 to 8

Cioppino, that classic seafood stew long associated with San Francisco though it hails from Italy, is like that little girl in Henry Wadsworth Longfellow's nursery rhyme: There was a little girl who had a little curl right in the middle of her forehead. When she was good, she was very, very good, but when she was bad, she was horrid.

A bad cioppino, and I've had many, really is horrid, with thick, gloppy tomato sauce and overcooked seafood. But when it is made properly, it is heavenly, a lusty rustic celebration of the sea. In California, we make it in the winter because that is when Dungeness crab is in season and so use either frozen tomato concassé or canned tomatoes. This dish illustrates so clearly how the specific tomatoes used impact the overall result. Use out-of-season tomatoes, tomato paste, commercial tomato sauce, or canned tomatoes that include other ingredients and you'll have a vastly different result than when you use either tomato concassé or a superior brand of diced organic tomatoes.

3 tablespoons olive oil

1 yellow onion, cut into small dice

1 celery rib, minced

6 to 8 garlic cloves, crushed and minced

Kosher salt

2 cups dry white wine

1 bay leaf

½ teaspoon red pepper flakes

1 tablespoon fresh minced oregano or 1 teaspoon dried oregano

1 teaspoon fresh thyme leaves or ½ teaspoon dried thyme

4 cups Tomato Concassé (page 263) or 28-ounce can diced tomatoes, preferably Muir Glen brand

1 cup minced fresh Italian parsley

3 Dungeness crabs, cooked and cleaned

3 pounds small clams or cockles, thoroughly washed

2 pounds black mussels, trimmed, if needed, and thoroughly washed

2 pounds wild prawns, headed and deveined

Black pepper in a mill

Sourdough bread, hot

Extra-virgin olive oil, preferably Davero Olio Nuovo

1 lemon, cut in wedges

Pour the olive oil into a large, heavy soup pot or Dutch oven set over medium-low heat. Add the onion and celery and sauté until soft and fragrant, about 10 to 12 minutes. Add the garlic, sauté 1 minute more, and season with salt. Add the white wine and stir in the pepper flakes, oregano, thyme, and tomatoes.

Increase the heat to high, bring to a boil, and immediately reduce the heat to very low; simmer for 15 minutes. Taste and correct for salt. Stir in the parsley.

Meanwhile, break apart the crab if you have not already done so; break the body into four pieces and separate the segments of the legs and claws. Sort through the clams or cockles and the mussels to remove any that don't close tightly, that are obviously empty (they will be very light), or that are filled with mud (these will be the ones that open very easily, without resistance).

Put the clams or cockles and the mussels into the pot, cover, and simmer over medium heat for 4 minutes. Add the crab and simmer 2 minutes. Stir in the prawns, cook for 1 minute, remove from the heat, and let rest, covered, for 5 minutes.

Taste the broth, correct for salt, and season generously with black pepper.

To serve, ladle into large soup bowls, making sure that each portion has a good mix of seafood. Drizzle with olive oil and serve immediately, with the hot bread, lemon wedges, and more olive oil alongside.

Rosefish Veracruz

Serves 3 to 4

This dish has two sources of inspiration, the classic Snapper Veracruz or Vercruzana, typically prepared with a whole snapper, and the little red perch, sometimes known as rosefish, that I love. There are many versions, some that call for a sauce prepared in advance, and others, including this one, that let the sauce form as the fish cooks. Traditional versions frequently include pickled jalapeños and some of their brine but I prepare this dish using fresh chilies and, for acid, fresh lime juice.

1½ pounds rosefish (red perch), dressed but whole
½ teaspoon chipotle powder
Kosher salt
Black pepper in a mill
Extra-virgin olive oil
1 yellow onion, peeled and very thinly sliced
5 garlic cloves, crushed and minced
2 to 3 ripe tomatoes, cored and cut into very thin rounds
2 to 3 bay leaves
1 poblano, seared, peeled, seeded, and cut into medium julienne

2 jalapeños, seared, peeled, seeded, and cut into small julienne
2 tablespoons capers
2 teaspoons dried Mexican oregano
1 medium tomato, peeled, cored, and minced
2 limes
½ cup pitted green olives, such as picholine, cut in half crosswise
Chopped cilantro
Steamed rice
Hot corn tortillas

Preheat the oven to 375°F.

Set the rosefish on a clean work surface and sprinkle the chipotle powder inside the cavities of the fish. Season the fish lightly all over with salt and pepper. Set aside.

Pour just enough olive oil into a heavy skillet—cast iron is perfect—to coat the bottom and spread the onions in the pan; scatter the garlic over the onions. Top with the tomatoes, tiling them over the surface of the entire pan. Top with the bay leaves and scatter half the jalapeños, half the capers, and half the oregano on top.

Arrange the rosefish on top and then scatter the remaining jalapeños, capers, and oregano over the fish. Drizzle some olive oil on the fish, squeeze the juice of 1 lime over everything, scatter the olives on top, and set in the oven.

Bake for about 15 minutes, until the fish is cooked through and the sauce is hot and bubbly.

Cut the remaining lime into wedges.

Transfer to a trivet or other protective surface.

Scatter cilantro on top and serve hot from the pan, with lime wedges, rice, and tortillas alongside.

Tomato Halibut Tagine

Serves 4

This tagine—as many Moroccan stews are called—is not traditional. It is entirely my own but it is inspired by Paula Wolfert and her extraordinary work on the foods of Morocco. It is also inspired by the cooking vessel known as a tagine, which consists of a flat container with slanted sides about two inches high and a round cover shaped like a chimney with a small opening. One of the major differences here is that I use poblano chilies instead of green bell peppers, which are common not just in Morocco but throughout the Mediterranean. I use them for a simple reason: I love them and they are abundant where I live in Northern California. They are, of course, traditionally used in Mexican cooking but I find they are quite delicious in this context, too. Feel free to use bell peppers if you like but do sear their skins and peel them first.

Red Chermoula (page 252)
1 pound wild Pacific halibut fillet
1 lemon, cut in half
Kosher salt
1 garlic clove, crushed
3 large beefsteak tomatoes, trimmed, cut into ¼-inch rounds
3 to 4 poblanos, roasted, peeled, and seeded
1 or 2 serranos, minced
Steamed couscous
Chopped cilantro, for garnish

Make the Chermoula up to a day before preparing the tagine.

A few hours before serving the tagine, set the halibut on a clean work surface, squeeze the juice of half the lemon over it, and sprinkle all over with salt. Let rest 10 to 15 minutes, rinse under cool water, and pat dry with a clean tea towel.

Cut the fish into four equal pieces and brush all over with some of the Chermoula. Set on a plate, cover, and refrigerate.

Remove the fish from the refrigerator at least 30 minutes before cooking.

Set the bottom part of a clay tagine on a work surface and rub it all over with the garlic.

Arrange the tomatoes over the bottom of the tagine and spoon about 3 tablespoons of Chermoula over them. Cut or tear the poblanos into wide strips and arrange them on top of the tomatoes. Scatter the serranos over the poblanos.

Set a heat diffuser over a medium-low burner and set the bottom of the tagine on top; cook gently until the tomatoes begin to fall apart, about 20 minutes.

Set the halibut on top of the vegetables and spoon about 3 tablespoons of Chermoula on top.

Add the top of the tagine and cook very gently until the halibut is just done, about 20 minutes for thick fillets.

While the tagine cooks, prepare the couscous and cut the remaining half lemon into wedges.

To serve, transfer the tagine to the table, setting it on a trivet or some other protective item. Add the couscous, remaining Chermoula, and lemon wedges alongside.

Summer Chicken Cacciatore

Serves 4

One of the most familiar Italian ways of preparing chicken, chicken cacciatore translates to "hunter's chicken," as it is said to be what a hunter's wife prepared for her husband
if he showed up empty-handed after a day of hunting. Most versions call for a whole chick-
en, cut into pieces, but I think it is best with dark meat and so I use leg-thighs or thighs.

4 chicken leg-thigh pieces or 8 thighs, preferably from pastured chickens
Kosher salt
Black pepper in a mill
2 tablespoons olive oil
1 large yellow onion, trimmed and thinly sliced lengthwise
3 to 4 garlic cloves, minced
1½ cups dry white wine
1 bay leaf
1 oregano sprig
2 thyme sprigs
3 or 4 large ripe tomatoes, peeled, cored, and chopped
1 roasted red bell pepper, peeled, seeded, and cut in medium julienne
3 tablespoons chopped fresh Italian parsley

Set the chicken on a clean work surface and season it all over with salt and
pepper.

Set a large sauté pan over medium heat, add the olive oil, and add the
chicken, being certain not to crowd it. Cook until the skin is nicely browned,
turn, and cook until browned on the other side. Transfer to a plate.

Add onion and sauté, stirring now and then, until softened, about 7 or 8
minutes. Add the garlic and sauté 2 minutes more; do not let the onions or
garlic brown.

Season with salt and pepper.

Add the white wine, bay leaf, oregano, and thyme and return the chicken
to the pan, along with any juices that have collected on the plate. When the

wine begins to simmer, reduce the heat, cover the pan, and cook gently for 20 minutes.

Uncover, increase the heat, and reduce the pan juices by two-thirds.

Add the tomatoes, agitate the pan to distribute them evenly, and cook until the tomatoes soften, about 10 to 15 minutes.

Use tongs to retrieve and discard the bay leaf and herb sprigs.

Add the roasted pepper, cover the pan, and cook for 5 minutes.

Carefully transfer the chicken to a serving platter, increase the heat to high, taste the pan juices, and correct for salt and pepper. When the pan juices have thickened a bit, pour them over the chicken, sprinkle the parsley on top, and serve.

Variation:
- To make this dish when tomatoes are not in season, cut 2 peeled carrots into medium julienne and add them to the pan with the onions. Add 8 to 10 ounces chanterelle mushrooms, cleaned, if available; otherwise use oyster mushrooms or sliced cremini mushrooms. Use a 28-ounce can of diced tomatoes in place of the fresh tomatoes. Omit the roasted pepper.

Ficandó
Catalan Veal Stew

Serves 6 to 8

I learned to make this dish when I was a guest at Catacurian, a tiny homestay cooking school in the mountains west of Barcelona. It had a fairly small but extremely efficient and beautiful kitchen, ideal for the four students who attended each session. This dish is an excellent example of the way tomatoes play a supporting yet essential role. You might not notice them immediately, but if they were left out, you'd know immediately that something was missing. If you do not want to use veal or find it hard to get, you can use pork shoulder or butt instead, as I usually do.

⅓ cup Picado (recipe follows)
2½ to 3 pounds boneless veal, cut into randomly sized slices
Kosher salt or Sel Gris
1 cup flour
4 tablespoons olive oil plus 3 tablespoons lard
3 shallots, thinly sliced lengthwise
1 onion, thinly sliced lengthwise
¾ cup dry vermouth or white wine
3 tomatoes, peeled, seeded, and minced (about 1 cup)
3 cups veal or beef stock
Bouquet garni of 1 bay leaf, 3 thyme sprigs, 1 3-inch celery stalk, 1-inch
    leek, white part only, wrapped and tied with kitchen twine
4 garlic cloves, minced
¾ pound golden chanterelles

First, make the Picado and set it aside.

Season the meat all over with salt and dredge it in flour, shaking off excess but being certain the meat is thoroughly coated.

In a large pot or a traditional Spanish cazuela set over a ring on top of a burner turned to medium heat, heat 3 tablespoons of the olive oil with the lard. When the mixture is hot, sauté the shallots and onion until limp. Season with salt, add the meat, and pour in the vermouth or white wine. Cook until the vermouth or wine is nearly completely evaporated. Stir in the tomatoes and beef stock and add the bouquet garni. Simmer, uncovered, until the meat is very tender, about 1 hour.

Add the Picado and cook until the juices have thickened, about 15 to 20 minutes.

When the *ficandó* is nearly done, pour the remaining olive oil in a sauté pan set over medium heat, add the garlic, and sauté 15 seconds. Add the mushrooms, season with salt, and sauté, stirring frequently, until the mushrooms are limp. If they remain firm, add a splash of vermouth or white wine, cover the pan, and cook for 3 minutes. Season with salt and stir into the stew.

Boeuf Bourguignonne
Classic Beef Stew

Serves 6 to 8

Cooked long and slow, Boeuf Bourguignonne is one of the most delicious beef dishes in the world. Serve it with a big green salad, with a Pinot Noir or a Côtes du Rhône alongside.

4 pounds beef chuck, cut into
    medium chunks
12 shallots, peeled
3 carrots, peeled and cut into small
    (¼-inch) dice
6 garlic cloves, peeled
2 parsley sprigs
2 thyme sprigs
1 bay leaf
1 bottle dry red wine
2 tablespoons butter

4 ounces pancetta or salt pork, diced
Kosher salt
Black pepper in a mill
¼ cup all-purpose flour
1 14-ounce can diced tomatoes
2 cups beef stock
1 pound very small white
    mushrooms, cleaned
2 tablespoons minced fresh parsley
1½ pounds small new potatoes

Put the beef, shallots, carrots, and garlic into a large, nonreactive bowl. Tie the parsley, thyme, and bay leaf together, add them to the bowl, and toss the ingredients together gently with your hands. Pour the wine over the mixture, cover tightly, and refrigerate overnight.

To cook the stew, remove the mixture from the refrigerator and use tongs to remove the chunks of meat. Pat the meat dry with a clean tea towel. Reserve the marinade.

Set a deep sauté pan over medium heat, add a tablespoon of the butter and the pancetta or salt pork, and fry until almost crisp, about 7 to 8 minutes.

Add the beef and season it all over with salt. Cook the meat until it is browned on all sides. Sprinkle the flour over it and season with several generous turns of black pepper.

                     A Tomato Cookbook

Pour the marinade, including the vegetables and bouquet garni, over the meat and add the tomatoes and stock. Bring to a boil and stir well with a wooden spoon, scraping up any bits of pancetta and beef that have stuck to the pan.

Reduce the heat to very low, cover, and simmer until the beef is tender, about 2½ hours. Add the mushrooms, stir, and cook 45 minutes more.

When you put the mushrooms in, fill a medium saucepan half full with water, add a tablespoon of salt, and bring to a boil over high heat. Peel the potatoes, add them to the water, and cook until tender when pierced with a bamboo skewer. Drain, put in a warm bowl, and toss with the remaining butter and the parsley. Cover and keep warm.

To serve, taste the stew and correct the seasoning. Use tongs to remove and discard the bouquet garni. Divide among warm soup plates, add potatoes alongside, and serve.

Beef, Cherry Tomatoes & Mushrooms on Skewers

Serves 6

If you love ginger, this simple dish will delight you. Although there are several necessary steps, the recipe is not difficult and does not take a lot of time. It also transports well, making it a good choice for a potluck.

2 pounds beef tenderloin, thinly sliced
1 cup dry red wine
Juice of 2 lemons
½ cup olive oil, plus more as needed
5 cloves garlic, crushed
4 slices fresh ginger, chopped
Kosher salt
Black pepper in a mill
3 medium red onions, trimmed and peeled
Olive oil
24 small to medium cremini mushrooms, tough stems removed
1 dozen 12-inch-long wooden skewers, soaked in water for at least 30 minutes
36 cherry tomatoes
1 bunch cilantro, rinsed and dried
Green Tomato and Onion Chutney (page 260), Tomato-Garlic Chutney(page 259), or Tomato-Onion Relish (page 257)

Put the sliced beef in a glass pan or other shallow, nonreactive container. Mix together the wine, lemon juice, olive oil, garlic, and ginger. Season generously with salt and several turns of black pepper. Pour half the marinade over the beef and set the rest aside. Turn the beef in the marinade to completely coat it. Cover and refrigerate for 1 to 3 hours.

Thirty minutes before assembling the skewers, remove the beef from the refrigerator.

Build a fire in an outdoor grill.

Brush the onions with olive oil, set them on the grill, and cook until they begin to soften, about 20 minutes; turn them now and then. Transfer to a plate, cool until easy to handle, and cut into quarters.

Heat a few tablespoons of the marinade in a sauté pan, add the mushrooms, and cook until they begin to soften, about 6 to 7 minutes. Remove from the heat and let cool.

To assemble the skewers, thread a strip of beef, 2 or 3 tomatoes, 2 mushrooms, and a generous piece of onion on each of the 12 skewers. Grill over medium coals for 2 to 3 minutes, turn, and grill 2 to 3 minutes more.

Cover a platter with the cilantro, set the skewers on top, and serve right away, with chutney or relish alongside.

Provençal-Style Leg of Lamb
with Onions, Potatoes, Tomatoes & Rosemary

Serves 6 to 8

As the lamb cooks, its juices bathe the vegetables beneath it, creating a rich, luscious flavor that permeates all the way into the potatoes. This is a special-occasion dish and I recommend beginning with a refreshing soup such as a gazpacho and ending with a big simple green salad.

1 whole leg of lamb, trimmed of the fell
3 cloves garlic, sliced
Kosher salt
Black pepper in a mill
2 to 3 tablespoons extra-virgin olive oil
2 pounds small new potatoes, cut into ¼-inch rounds
2 yellow onions, sliced
20 garlic cloves, peeled
¾ cup pitted black olives or green olives
6 to 8 large ripe tomatoes, stem ends removed, cut into ¼-inch-thick rounds
10 to 12 small rosemary sprigs
Flake salt

Preheat the oven to 400°F.

Use the tip of a sharp knife to make several slits in the lamb and tuck a piece of sliced garlic in each cut. Season the lamb all over with salt and pepper.

Pour enough olive oil into a roasting pan to completely coat the surface and arrange the potatoes in the pan, overlapping them just slightly. Spread the onions on top of the potatoes and scatter the garlic cloves and olives on top. Tuck 6 rosemary sprigs here and there and season all over with salt and pepper.

Tile the tomatoes on top and season lightly with salt and pepper.

Set a roasting rack on top of the vegetables and set the leg of lamb on the rack.

A Tomato Cookbook

Transfer to the middle rack of the oven and cook for 20 minutes.

Lower the heat to 325°F and cook until the lamb reaches an internal temperature of about 120°F or a little higher for medium-rare; it will take about 15 to 20 minutes per pound.

Remove from the oven, cover loosely with aluminum foil, and let rest 15 to 20 minutes.

Transfer the lamb to a clean work surface and carve it into fairly thin slices.

Use a large metal spatula to transfer the vegetables from the roasting pan to a serving platter; arrange the carved lamb alongside. Garnish with the remaining rosemary sprigs, sprinkle with salt and several turns of black pepper, and serve immediately.

Salsas & Other Condiments

Although the Spanish word salsa translates into English simply as "sauce" (*sals* is an obsolete form of English *sauce*), we think of salsa as a mildly to intensely spicy condiment typically associated with Mexican and other Latin American cooking and, to a lesser degree, Italian and Spanish cuisines. The chips-and-salsa duo sits on the tables of most Mexican restaurants, and market shelves are lined with scores of variations of the increasingly popular relish.

Many, even most, traditional salsas, as well as many innovative versions, begin with tomatoes—fresh ripe ones in season and canned tomatoes the rest of the year—or tomatillos, but the concept has been stretched to incorporate everything from watermelon, cherries, mangos, and bananas to pumpkin seeds, green olives, black beans, and minced clams. Made with good ingredients and the proper balance of heat, acid, and salt, nearly any mixture, however unusual, can be wonderful, though I prefer not to deviate too far from the original tradition. There's a point at which a salsa should be called something else.

Salsas are most often rough textured, with the ingredients cut into small to medium dice, but several traditional Mexican salsas are smooth or nearly so. In Mexico and beyond, salsas are used as condiments with egg, fish, poultry, meat, cheese, and rice dishes and, of course, on tacos. You find similar condiments, naturally under other names, including the Red Chimichurri and Red Chermoula you'll find in this chapter, in Africa, India, the Middle East, and the Mediterranean, anywhere that peasant foods are flavorful and robust and where there are plenty of fresh vegetables available.

Throughout America, there are dozens of tomato-based condiments, from simple tomato butter and our classic ketchup, now used around the world, to tomato jelly, tomato jam, relishes, chutneys, and more.

Pico de Gallo
Salsa Cruda
Yellow Tomato Salsa
Green Shiso Salsa
Tomato Butter
Red Chimichurri
Red Chermoula
Pistou
Tomato Ketchup
Spicy Tomato Jelly
Tomato-Onion Relish
Tomato-Currant Chutney
Tomato-Garlic Chutney
Green Tomato & Onion Chutney

Pico de Gallo

Makes about 2 cups

This is the simplest and one of the most common of the traditional Mexican salsas. Made with ripe tomatoes it is as good with chips and tacos as it is with rice, beans, and grilled meats.

4 to 5 ripe red tomatoes, cored, cut into small dice
1 small white onion, cut into small dice
2 or 3 serranos, stemmed and minced
½ cup cilantro leaves, chopped
Kosher salt

In a medium bowl, toss together the tomatoes, onion, peppers, and cilantro. Add salt to taste and let the mixture rest at least 30 minutes before serving.

Salsa Cruda

Makes 1¾ to 2 cups

This salsa has a bit more structure and depth of flavor than Pico de Gallo and it is my default version when I'm craving salsa and chips.

2 cups Tomato Concassé
1 small white onion, cut into small dice
3 or 4 cloves garlic, crushed and minced
2 to 3 serranos, stemmed and minced
2 tablespoons tomato purée
Juice of ½ lemon
2 tablespoons medium-acid red wine vinegar
Kosher salt
Black pepper in a mill
¼ cup extra-virgin olive oil
½ cup cilantro leaves, chopped
1 tablespoon minced fresh oregano leaves

Put the Tomato Concassé into a bowl, add the onion, garlic, and serranos, and toss together. Stir in the tomato purée, lemon juice, and vinegar. Season with salt and pepper, stir in the olive oil, and add the cilantro and oregano.

Correct for salt and pepper, cover, and let rest 30 minutes before serving.

Yellow Tomato Salsa

Makes about 3 cups

Delicate and pleasing to both the eye and the palate, this light salsa is lovely on poached chicken, grilled fish and shellfish, green beans and roasted potatoes. It is also excellent in tacos filled with sautéed zucchini.

2 cups small yellow tomatoes, quartered
1 small torpedo onion, minced
2 cloves garlic, minced
1 serrano, minced
Juice of 1 lemon
Kosher salt
Black pepper in a mill
½ cup extra-virgin olive oil
¼ cup cilantro leaves, chopped

Put the tomatoes into a small bowl, add the onion, garlic, serrano, and lemon juice, and season with salt and pepper. Stir in the olive oil, add the cilantro, taste, and correct for salt. Cover and set aside for 30 minutes before serving.

Green Shiso Salsa

Makes about 1½ cups

Not all green tomatoes are unripe. Some have been bred for their color and many green tomatoes, such as the Green Zebra, are more acidic than most red tomatoes. When you can get good ripe green tomatoes, try this lovely salsa, which is excellent on seafood, especially ahi tuna grilled rare.

1 pound Green Zebra or Evergreen tomatoes, cored and cut into small dice
4 to 5 scallions, trimmed and cut in small rounds
1 serrano, stemmed and minced
4 cloves of garlic, peeled, crushed, and minced
2 to 3 tablespoons minced cilantro leaves
1 tablespoon minced shiso leaf
1 tablespoon rice wine vinegar
Juice of 1 lime
Kosher salt

Put the tomatoes into a small bowl, add the scallions, serrano, garlic, cilantro, and minced shiso leaf. Stir in the vinegar and lime juice and add salt to taste. Season with a little black pepper, cover, and set aside for 30 minutes before serving.

Tomato Butter

Makes about ½ cup

Use tomato butter with biscuits and scones, grilled seafood and chicken, or tossed with pasta as a light side dish. It is also excellent with a wide array of vegetables, especially grilled zucchini, steamed broccoli, broccoli rabe, steamed carrots, and baked potatoes.

2 ripe tomatoes (about ½ cup pulp), peeled, seeded, and finely chopped
1 shallot, minced
¼ cup butter (1 stick), softened and cut in pieces
Kosher salt and freshly ground black pepper
1 tablespoon snipped fresh chives or 1 tablespoon finely minced Italian
   parsley (optional)

Let the tomatoes drain in a fine sieve for about 15 minutes, and reserve the drained liquid for another use. Transfer the remaining tomato pulp and shallot to a food processor and pulse briefly to blend. Add the butter and pulse until the mixture is smooth. Add a generous pinch of salt and healthy sprinkling of pepper, along with the chives or parsley if using. Store the tomato butter in the refrigerator in a glass bowl or jar, covered, for 3 or 4 days. Let it sit at room temperature for about 30 minutes before using.

Red Chimichurri

Makes about 1¼ cups

Chimichurri is as ubiquitous in Argentina as ketchup is in America. In restaurants, it always accompanies steak and most other meats. There are many versions, some without tomatoes, and others, like this one, with tomatoes.

4 to 5 large garlic cloves, crushed
Kosher salt
1 small shallot, chopped
½ cup chopped fresh Italian parsley
¼ cup chopped fresh cilantro
1 tablespoon fresh oregano
1 medium ripe tomato, peeled, seeded, minced, and drained
1 gypsy pepper, seared, peeled, seeded, and minced
1 tablespoon smoked Spanish paprika
A few pinches of crushed red pepper, chipotle powder, or piment d'Espelette
¼ cup red wine vinegar
⅓ to ½ cup extra-virgin olive oil
Black pepper in a mill

Put the garlic into a suribachi, sprinkle with salt, and use a wooden pestle to grind to a paste. Add the shallot and pound and grind into the garlic.

Using a rubber spatula, fold the parsley, cilantro, and oregano into the paste. Stir in the tomato and gypsy pepper, add the paprika and hot pepper of choice, and stir in the vinegar and olive oil.

Add several turns of black pepper, taste, and correct for salt and acid.

Red Chermoula

As chermoula, a traditional Moroccan condiment, has become increasingly popular in the United States, you see more and more versions, some with preserved lemons, some with roasted sweet peppers, and some, like this one, with fresh tomatoes. The most important elements are the proper balance of acid and enough spices. When it all comes together perfectly, as if by alchemy, it can be one of the best things you have ever tasted. Chermoula is excellent with sausages, bread salad, soup, grilled and roasted seafood, poultry and meat, and, simply, over plain yogurt.

3 garlic cloves, crushed
Kosher salt
1 teaspoon hot Spanish paprika
1 teaspoon sweet Spanish paprika
1 teaspoon ground cumin
1 teaspoon piment d'Espelette or chipotle powder
Juice of 1 lemon, plus more to taste

½ cup chopped fresh Italian parsley
½ cup chopped fresh cilantro
3 small red tomatoes, such as Early Girl or Shady Lady, cored and cut into small dice
Black pepper in a mill
½ cup best-quality extra-virgin olive oil, plus more to taste

Put the garlic into a suribachi or large mortar, sprinkle with salt, and use a wooden pestle to grind it into a paste. Add the paprikas, cumin, and piment d'Espelette or chipotle powder and the lemon juice. Stir and season with several generous pinches of salt.

Add the parsley and cilantro and pound it just a bit to incorporate it into the garlic and spices.

Use a rubber spatula to fold in the tomatoes. Taste, correct for salt, and season with several turns of black pepper.

Add the olive oil and taste for acid balance, adding more lemon juice or more olive oil as needed.

Use immediately or store in the refrigerator, covered, for up to 3 or 4 days.

Pistou

Makes about 2 cups

Pistou, which is the Provençal equivalent of pesto, is typically served with soupe au pistou, a summer vegetable and bean soup not unlike minestrone. It is delicious on almost any summer tomato soup and is a perfect solution to dinner on a busy night, when you can simply toss it with pasta.

5 large garlic cloves
Kosher salt
Black pepper in a mill
5 cups fresh basil leaves, torn into pieces
2 tomatoes, peeled, seeded, and minced
½ cup extra-virgin olive oil
3 ounces Dry Jack, grated

In a large, heavy mortar or in the bowl of a suribachi, use a wooden pestle to crush each clove of garlic. Add several generous pinches of salt and several turns of pepper and pound the garlic until it is smooth. Add the basil, a small handful at a time, and continue to pound until the basil is crushed and incorporated into the pistou.

Fold in the tomato and stir in the olive oil and cheese. Taste and correct for salt and pepper. Cover and set aside or refrigerate until ready to use.

Tomato Ketchup

Makes about 3 pints

Today, ketchup is synonymous with tomatoes but it hasn't always been that way. One of the first recorded versions was made with mushrooms, another with walnuts; go back even further in history and you'll find all manner of fish and shellfish among the ingredients. Because no book on tomatoes would be complete without a recipe for America's classic condiment, here's my version.

10 pounds ripe plum tomatoes, peeled, seeded, chopped, and drained
2 yellow onions, peeled and chopped
1 head garlic, cloves separated, peeled, and chopped
2 cups apple cider vinegar
2 cups brown sugar, packed
1 tablespoon hot mustard flour (or Colman's dry mustard) mixed with cold
   water to make a paste
2 3-inch pieces of cinnamon
1 teaspoon crushed red pepper flakes
1 tablespoon whole black peppercorns
½ nutmeg, crushed
5 or 6 cardamom seeds or 1 cardamom pod, broken open
1 teaspoon whole cloves
1 teaspoon whole juniper berries
2 teaspoons fennel seeds
3 sprigs fresh Italian parsley
Kosher salt

Put the tomatoes in a large, heavy pot, add the onions and garlic, and bring to a boil over medium heat, stirring now and then so that the tomatoes do not burn. Reduce the heat and simmer very gently for 25 to 30 minutes, until the tomatoes are completely soft.

Remove the tomatoes from the heat and let cool for about 5 minutes. Pass the mixture through a food mill, discard any remaining solids, and return the purée to the cleaned pot. Stir in the vinegar, sugar, and mustard paste.

Cut a 6-inch square of cheesecloth, set the cinnamon, red pepper flakes, peppercorns, nutmeg, cardamom, cloves, juniper berries, and fennel seed in the center of the square and tie it closed with a piece of kitchen twine. Submerge it in the tomato mixture and add the parsley sprigs.

Simmer over extremely low heat until the ketchup is thick and fragrant, about 2½ to 3 hours. Check periodically, skim off any foam that forms on the surface, and stir so that the ketchup does not scorch.

Remove from the heat and let cool. Use tongs to remove and discard the bag of spices.

Ladle the ketchup into scalded half-pint or pint jars, store in the refrigerator, or process in a water bath.

Spicy Tomato Jelly

Makes 5 half pints

A spicy-sweet jelly is a delightful accompaniment to many dishes—both sweet and savory. This one's great on toast, too, or with the scones on page 146.

2 cups Tomato Essence (page 267)
½ cup fresh lemon juice
3 cups sugar
2 or 3 serranos, scored to reveal interior (more or less, to taste)
1 2-inch piece of cinnamon
1 2-inch piece of vanilla bean
3 ounces liquid pectin

In a large, nonreactive pot, combine the Tomato Essence, lemon juice, sugar, peppers, cinnamon, and vanilla bean. Bring the mixture to a rolling boil and remove from the heat. Let the mixture sit for 1 hour. Discard the peppers, cinnamon, and vanilla bean. Return the tomato mixture to the heat and return it to a full boil. Add the pectin, boil 1 minute, stirring constantly, and remove from the heat. Skim off any foam that has formed on the top, ladle the jelly into scalded half-pint jars, add lids and rings, and process in a water bath for 5 minutes.

Remove the jars from the water bath, cool them, check the seals, and store the jars in a cool, dark cupboard until ready to use.

Tomato-Onion Relish

I love sweet onions nearly as much as I love tomatoes; I can never get enough of them when they are in season, so here's a way of preserving their flavor.

3 large sweet onions (Walla Walla, Maui, or other sweet onion)
Olive oil
2 cups roasted tomatoes
½ cup golden raisins, soaked in ½ cup sherry vinegar or apple cider vinegar
Kosher salt and freshly ground black pepper

Peel the onions and cut them in half. Brush them with olive oil and grill them either over open coals or on a stovetop grill, or roast them in a 325°F oven until they are soft and tender, about 20 to 25 minutes.

Let the onions cool.

Set a strainer over a deep bowl, add the roasted tomatoes, and let their liquid drain into the bowl; reserve it for another purpose. Chop the tomato pulp and place it in a large porcelain or stainless-steel bowl. Drain the raisins and add them to the tomato pulp, along with 3 tablespoons of the vinegar. Coarsely chop the onions, add them to the tomatoes, and toss.

Taste the relish and season with salt and pepper. This relish will keep refrigerated for about 2 weeks.

Tomato-Currant Chutney

Makes 4 to 5 pints

This chutney—based on canned tomatoes—was developed out of impatience. It was the middle of winter; I wanted some tomato chutney. I decided to experiment with various canned products and was pleased with the results using Muir Glen diced tomatoes.

1 pound Zante currants
3 cups apple cider vinegar
¾ pound brown sugar
1 2-inch piece of cinnamon
4 allspice berries
½ teaspoon nutmeg
¼ teaspoon cardamom seeds

½ teaspoon cumin seeds, toasted
1 teaspoon hot red pepper flakes
3 tablespoons olive oil
1 medium yellow onion, minced
8 cloves garlic, minced
1 28-ounce can diced or ground
    tomatoes

Place the currants in a wide, heavy saucepan, cover them with the vinegar, and bring the liquid to a simmer over medium heat. Remove it from the fire, stir in the brown sugar and all the spices, and let the mixture rest for 30 minutes. Heat the olive oil in a heavy skillet and sauté the onion until it is soft and transparent, about 15 minutes. Add the garlic and sauté another 2 minutes. Add the onion and garlic combination to the currant and spice mixture, place the pan over medium heat, and simmer the liquid until most of it has evaporated and the mixture has begun to thicken. Add the tomatoes, stir, simmer 15 minutes, and remove from the heat. Spoon into hot, sterilized half-pint or pint jars to within a half inch of the rim and seal jar according to manufacturer's directions. Process for 15 minutes in a boiling water bath. Store in a cool, dark cupboard for up to 1 year. You may also store the chutney in the refrigerator for up to 3 weeks.

Tomato-Garlic Chutney

Makes about 1 quart

Before making this simple yet full-flavored chutney, be sure to read about preserving tomatoes on page 281. Use this condiment with traditional curries, on sandwiches, and with grilled meats.

¾ cup fresh sliced garlic (about 2 heads)
2 serrano peppers, stemmed and finely minced
4 tablespoons minced fresh ginger
1 cup brown sugar
1 cup apple cider vinegar
½ cup balsamic vinegar
1 1-inch piece of cinnamon
1 teaspoon crushed red pepper
4 cups fresh chopped tomatoes
1 teaspoon kosher salt

Place the garlic, minced peppers, ginger, sugar, vinegars, cinnamon, and red pepper in a heavy, nonreactive pot, stir to blend well, and simmer the mixture over medium heat for about 30 minutes, until the garlic is tender and the liquid is reduced by half. Stir in the tomatoes and the salt, reduce the heat, and simmer the chutney until it thickens, about 25 minutes. Remove the chutney from heat and spoon it into hot, sterilized half-pint or pint jars to within a quarter inch of the rim and seal according to manufacturer's directions. Process for 15 minutes in a boiling water bath. Store in a cool, dark cupboard for up to 1 year or in the refrigerator for up to 3 weeks.

Green Tomato & Onion Chutney

Makes 10 to 12 pints

If you grow tomatoes, you invariably end up with green tomatoes when the first frost hits. Try to anticipate it and harvest the tomatoes, because a frost can turn them mushy.

8 pounds unripe green tomatoes, free of blemishes, cored and cut into thin rounds

2 pounds yellow onions, trimmed, peeled, and cut into thin rounds

1 tablespoon kosher salt, plus more as needed

2 pounds currants

4 cups apple cider vinegar

1 garlic bulb, cloves separated, peeled, and minced

3 to 4 serranos or jalapeños, stemmed and minced, plus more to taste

⅓ cup freshly grated ginger

3 pounds brown sugar

Put the sliced tomatoes and sliced onions in a large bowl, toss together gently, and sprinkle with salt. Cover and set aside overnight.

Put the currants into a medium bowl, add the vinegar, and set aside overnight.

To finish the chutney, drain the juices off the tomatoes and onions and put them into a large pot. Add the currants and vinegar, the garlic, the serranos or jalapeños, the ginger, and the brown sugar and set over medium heat. Stir gently now and then until the liquid is very hot and the sugar is dissolved. Skim off any foam that rises to the surface.

Reduce the heat to low and cook for 3 hours, stirring now and then, until it is very thick and clear.

While the chutney cooks, sterilize pint jars and their seals and lids and keep them hot.

When the chutney is done, set the hot jars on a folded tea towel and fill them, leaving about a quarter inch of headroom at the top. Seal and process in a hot water bath.

Cool, check the seals, and store in a dark pantry or cupboard for up to a year. Refrigerate after opening.

Classic & Contemporary
Tomato Sauces

The recipes in this section are my versions of traditional tomato sauces from France, Italy, and Mexico, along with a few that took shape over the years in my own kitchen without an antecedent. Some, especially tomato concassé and tomato coulis, are essential building blocks in other recipes, although they can also stand alone, as simple sauces for quick meals.

Others are complete in themselves and require only a vehicle—pasta, rice, polenta, an omelet, a tamale—to make a complete meal.

Spicy Tomato Mignonette
Tomato Concassé
Red Tomato Coulis
Golden Tomato Coulis
Fresh Tomato Sauce with Butter
Tomato Essence
Smoked Tomato Sauce
Winter Marinara
Winter Spaghetti Sauce with Beef
An Almost Traditional Ragù
Tomato Sauce with Hot Pepper & Pancetta
Mexican-Style Summer Tomato Sauce
Winter Tomato Sauce with Onions, Sage & Pancetta
Tomato-Lemon Sauce
Dried-Tomato Cream Sauce
Warm Cherry Tomato Vinaigrette

Spicy Tomato Mignonette

Makes about ½ to ¾ cup

Think of this delicate sauce, perfect for two to three dozen small oysters on the half shell, as tomato concassé in reverse. The process is the same, as you will see in the next recipe, but for mignonette, you use the juices that drain from the tomatoes, not the pulp that is left behind, which you should reserve for another dish. Yuzu is a citrus fruit native to Japan that is slowly becoming available in the United States.

2 to 3 large beefsteak tomatoes, minced
Kosher salt
1 small shallot, minced
1 small serrano or other hot chili, stemmed, seeded, and minced
2 tablespoons freshly squeezed lime or yuzu juice
2 tablespoons chopped cilantro leaves
Black pepper in a mill

Set a strainer over a deep bowl, put the minced tomatoes into it, season lightly with salt, and stir. Let drain, stirring now and then, for 30 minutes.

Meanwhile, put the shallot and chili into a small bowl, add the lime or yuzu juice, and set aside.

Reserve the drained pulp for another use and tip the tomato juices into the bowl with the shallot.

Taste, correct for salt, stir in the cilantro, and season very generously with black pepper.

Tomato Concassé

Makes about 2½ cups

Tomato concassé is a classic building block of countless traditional and innovative dishes. It refers, simply, to tomatoes that have been peeled, seeded, and chopped or minced. You'll find it in a line cook's setup—mise en place, "put in place"—and it is becoming increasingly common in the repertoire of home cooks. Don't be put off by the French term; it is just a quick way to say "tomatoes that have been peeled, seeded, chopped, and, frequently, drained of their excess juices."

Depending on the type of tomatoes you use, you will get between 1 cup and 1¼ cups per pound of tomatoes. It is best to use a beefsteak variety, as they have small seed pockets and typically yield more flesh than other varieties. Early Girl and Shady Lady are also good choices.

2 pounds red ripe beefsteak tomatoes
Kosher salt to taste

Peel the tomatoes by placing one at a time on the end of a fork and holding it over a high flame or hot burner to quickly sear the skin. Repeat until all tomatoes have been seared.

Use your fingers to peel off the skin, starting with the first tomato seared, as it will have cooled sufficiently.

Cut out the stem cores and cut the tomatoes in half through their equators.

Set a strainer over a deep bowl and gently squeeze out the gel and seeds. Stir the gel now and then so that it releases its juice. Tip the juice into a glass or other container and set aside. Discard the seeds.

Mince the tomatoes by hand as finely as possible and transfer them to the strainer. Add a generous pinch of salt and let drain for 20 to 30 minutes, stirring now and then.

Add the juice to the original juice and keep for other use.

Use the concassé right away or transfer to a container, cover, and refrigerate for 2 to 3 days.

Red Tomato Coulis

Makes about 4 to 6 cups

A coulis is a smooth sauce, thick yet pourable, and used both as a base for other dishes—soups, for example—or on its own. It is nowhere near as thick as tomato paste. This coulis freezes well and is a great way to preserve garden tomatoes if you are lucky enough to have them.

6 pounds ripe tomatoes, peeled, seeded, and chopped
1 tablespoon sugar
3 tablespoons olive oil
2 yellow onions, peeled and chopped
2 teaspoons minced garlic
5 basil leaves, finely chopped
Several sprigs Italian parsley
1 bay leaf
Kosher salt and freshly ground black pepper

Bring tomatoes and sugar to boil in a nonreactive stockpot. Simmer for 10 minutes and then transfer the tomatoes to a fine strainer lined with cheesecloth. Let excess liquid drain for 10 minutes and reserve it for another use. Return the drained tomato pulp to the pot and simmer over low heat until all the liquid has evaporated. Meanwhile, heat the olive oil in a heavy skillet and sauté the onions until they are soft and fragrant, about 10 minutes. Add the garlic, basil, parsley, and bay leaf and sauté another 2 minutes. Stir in the cooked tomato pulp. Taste the sauce and add salt and pepper as needed. For a completely smooth sauce, pass the sauce through a food mill. This sauce will keep, properly refrigerated, for up to a week and it can be frozen.

Golden Tomato Coulis

Makes about 2 cups

Golden tomatoes are often more flavorful than red ones, with both an intensity and delicacy that should be highlighted, as in this recipe.

6 ripe gold or yellow tomatoes
2 tablespoons (about ¾ ounce) butter
2 tablespoons minced shallots
Kosher salt and freshly ground black pepper
1 tablespoon minced fresh basil
1 tablespoon minced fresh Italian parsley
1 tablespoon fresh snipped chives

Peel the tomatoes by placing one at a time on the end of a fork and holding it over a gas flame to quickly sear the skin. Repeat until all tomatoes have been seared, let them rest and cool, and then remove the skins and stem cores. Cut each tomato in half horizontally and gently squeeze out the seeds and gel. Chop the tomatoes by hand very finely and set them aside.
Heat the butter in a heavy skillet and sauté the shallots in butter for 2 minutes; do not brown. Add tomato pulp and cook over moderate heat for several minutes until juices have evaporated and sauce thickens. Strain or pass through a food mill. Season with salt and pepper and stir in the herbs.

Fresh Tomato Sauce
with Butter

Makes about 2 cups

This is the simplest of the classic Italian tomato sauces. Fortified with butter, it is both rich and delicate, best served with simple pastas, such as pappardelle, fettuccine, handmade ravioli, and classic potato gnocchi. Just be sure to top the finished dish with a healthy grating of imported Parmigiano cheese.

6 tablespoons unsalted butter
1 yellow onion, peeled and chopped
10 to 12 ripe Roma tomatoes, cored, peeled, and seeded
Kosher salt

Heat the butter in a heavy skillet and sauté the onions over medium heat until they are soft and fragrant, being careful not to let them or the butter brown. While the onions cook, chop the tomatoes. Add them to the onions and cook together until the tomatoes are soft and have begun to give up their liquid, about 20 minutes. Remove them from the heat and pass the sauce through a food mill. (For a sauce with more texture, do not use the food mill.) Season to taste with salt. Serve the sauce immediately or store it in the refrigerator for up to 3 days.

Tomato Essence

Makes about 3 cups

This thin, fragrant liquid is intensely flavored and perfect when you want a lot of tomato flavor without a lot of texture. You will net about ¼ cup of tomato essence for every pound of tomatoes used, so judge your proportions by the amount of essence you need. I make mine most frequently in ten-pound batches. Be sure to begin with tomatoes that have good, balanced flavor.

10 pounds very ripe red tomatoes, cored and coarsely chopped

Purée the tomatoes using a food mill; discard the seeds and skins. Place the purée in a large, nonreactive pot and reduce it over medium heat by one-half, being sure not to scorch the liquid. Strain the reduced tomatoes through a fine sieve or a strainer lined with several layers of cheesecloth. Clean the pot and return the strained liquid to it. Reduce the mixture again until you have about 4 cups. Let the Tomato Essence cool, taste it, and if it seems at all weak or watery, reduce again by one-half. Cool and refrigerate for up to a week. This essence may also be frozen.

Smoked Tomato Sauce

Makes about 1 quart

    These days, many people have small, commercial smokers, and if you have one, follow the manufacturer's instructions. If you don't have one, you can make smoked tomatoes by using any outdoor barbecue fitted with a cover. Tomatoes take the flavor of smoke beautifully, and sauces and soups made with smoked tomatoes have an added dimension that is quite delicious.

Hickory chips or other wood chips, soaked in water
2 tablespoons pure olive oil
5 pounds Roma tomatoes, clean but left whole
1 small yellow onion, minced
3 sprigs Italian parsley
Kosher salt and freshly ground black pepper

Prepare a charcoal fire at least an hour before you wish to begin smoking your tomatoes. Brush the grill rack with olive oil. When the fire has cooled considerably from its peak of heat and the coals are completely covered with a thick coating of white ash, scatter the wet chips over the surface and the coals and quickly set the rack over the coals. The moistened chips should produce a large amount of smoke. Keep in mind that you are smoking rather than cooking these tomatoes, so make sure the fire is not too hot and that there is enough smoke being produced. Add more moistened chips if necessary.

Set the tomatoes on the grill, cover the barbecue, and close the vent on the lid nearly all the way. Check the tomatoes in about 45 minutes. They should be slightly shriveled with split skins. If they appear done, carefully transfer them to a large bowl or pan and set them aside to cool. If necessary, leave them on the grill, covered, for an additional 15 minutes.

When the tomatoes are easy to handle, remove and discard their skins, cores, and seeds, reserving all the juices. (At this point, you can store the tomatoes in the refrigerator for up to 1 week and in the freezer for up to 3 months.)

To finish the sauce, chop the pulp coarsely and pass it through a food mill. Heat the olive oil in a heavy skillet and sauté the onion until it is soft and fragrant, 15 to 20 minutes. Stir in the smoked tomato purée, add the parsley, lower the heat, and simmer the sauce for 15 to 20 minutes, until it just begins to thicken. Remove and discard the parsley sprigs, taste, and season with salt and pepper.

Serve the sauce with grilled seafood, sautéed scallops, grilled chicken, or barbecued ribs.

Winter Marinara

There's something arbitrary, almost unnecessary, about a recipe for spaghetti sauce. Certainly, don't use mine to supplant your own. But if, for whatever reason, you've never made what is correctly called marinara, this is a good way to start. Although the wine is optional, it adds a pleasant depth of flavor, welcome if the tomatoes you are using are not the best. For years, I used red wine but have since switched to white, as I prefer the way it lets the flavor of the tomatoes shine through.

Olive oil
1 medium yellow onion, diced
Several cloves of garlic, minced
¾ cup dry white wine, optional
Kosher salt
2 28-ounce cans of crushed tomatoes
1 very small handful of fresh oregano, finely chopped

2 or 3 tablespoons chopped fresh Italian parsley
Black pepper in a mill
l teaspoon sugar
1 to 3 tablespoons of tomato paste, as needed

Heat some olive oil in a heavy skillet set over medium heat. Add the onion and sauté it until soft and fragrant, about 10 to 12 minutes. Add the garlic and sauté 2 minutes more. Add the wine, if using, and simmer until it is reduced by half.

Season with salt.

Add the tomatoes, stir, add the oregano and parsley, and cook gently for about 15 minutes. Taste, correct for salt, and season with several turns of black pepper. If the tomatoes seem too acidic, stir in the sugar.

If the sauce is too thin, add tomato paste, a tablespoon at a time, to reach the desired consistency.

Simmer 10 minutes and remove from the heat. This sauce will keep in the refrigerator for up to 1 week; it can also be frozen for up to 3 months.

Winter Spaghetti Sauce
with Beef

Makes about 4 cups

This is the tomato sauce that I grew up on, the sauce my mother would make—without the wine—on Halloween because she knew I'd eat it, and the sauce I crave when I'm recovering from a bad cold or flu.

3 tablespoons pure olive oil
1 small yellow onion, peeled and cut into small dice
6 cloves garlic, peeled and minced
1 pound lean ground beef
Kosher salt
1 cup red wine
1 28-ounce can crushed or diced plum tomatoes, with their juice
Handful Italian parsley, chopped
Black pepper in a mill

Heat the olive oil in a heavy skillet, add the chopped onion, and sauté over medium heat until it is soft and transparent. Add the garlic and sauté 1 minute more. Add the beef and crumble it with a fork as it cooks, stirring continuously until it has lost its raw color. Season with salt.

Add the wine, increase the heat, and cook until it has nearly completely evaporated. Add the tomatoes, lower the heat, and simmer until most of the liquid has evaporated, about 30 minutes. If the sauce is fairly thin, raise the heat to medium and simmer an additional 5 minutes to thicken it. Stir in the parsley, taste, correct for salt, and season with several turns of black pepper.

Use right away or store, covered, in the refrigerator for 4 to 5 days.

A Tomato Cookbook

An Almost Traditional Ragù

Serves 6 to 8

Because so many commercial tomato sauces are called "ragù," Americans tend to think that's what a ragù is, a tomato sauce for pasta. Yet a traditional Italian ragù may not contain any tomatoes at all; rather, it is a sauce of meat, poultry, or a combination of the two, with finely diced vegetables and one or more liquids—water, milk, cream, wine, broth, or stock—simmered together for several hours. When tomatoes do appear, it tends to be in the form of a bit of tomato paste, which adds a deep layer of flavor, as you see in my version, which is almost but not quite traditional. It is best in the darkest winter months, when its preparation is a lovely balm against the elements. If the required dicing seems daunting to you, use a well-sharpened chef's knife and turn up your favorite music. It's a lovely way to spend a rainy morning.

3 to 3½ pounds chuck roast
3 tablespoons butter
3 tablespoons olive oil
8 ounces prosciutto or pancetta, cut into ¼-inch dice
2 yellow onions, cut into ¼-inch dice
3 to 4 carrots, peeled and cut into ⅛- to ¼-inch dice
3 to 4 celery stalks, cut into ⅛- to ¼-inch dice
Kosher salt
1½ cups dry white wine
3 tablespoons double-concentrated tomato paste
3 cups beef or poultry stock
1 cup half-and-half
Black pepper in a mill
½ cup minced fresh Italian parsley
1 cup heavy cream
3 to 4 garlic cloves, pressed

Use a sharp knife to cut the meat into about ¼- to ½-inch dice. To do so, cut the meat into crosswise slices, cut the slices in half lengthwise, and cut the slices into small pieces. Do not trim away the fat. Put the diced meat in a container and set aside.

Put the butter and olive oil into a wide, deep pot set over medium heat and when the butter is melted, add the diced prosciutto or pancetta and cook for about 5 minutes, stirring frequently. Add the onions and cook until limp, about 7 minutes. Add the carrots and celery, stir, and cook until all of the vegetables are soft, about 10 minutes more. Season with salt.

Add the diced beef and cook gently until it loses its raw look.

Add the wine, increase the heat to high, and cook until the wine is nearly completely reduced. Season with salt.

Stir the tomato paste into the stock and pour the mixture into the pot. When the mixture boils, add a splash of half-and-half and lower the heat so that the liquid barely simmers.

Cook for about 3½ hours, or until the meat is very tender and the liquid reduced. As the ragù cooks, add a splash of half-and-half and stir every 15 minutes or so. When the ragù is very thick, remove it from the heat and let it rest for a while, during which time fat will collect on its surface. Use a wide spoon to scoop off and discard this fat.

At this point, the ragù is ready to be reheated and served. To do so, pour the cream into a small saucepan, add the pressed garlic, and simmer until the cream is reduced by half. Strain it directly into the ragù, stir, and reheat.

Best Uses: With papardelle, bucatini, or fusilli col buco; with creamy polenta; in traditional lasagne.

Tomato Sauce
with Hot Pepper & Pancetta

Makes about 3 cups

This traditional Italian pasta sauce is very appealing in its spicy simplicity. Notice that garlic is not among the ingredients. Many Italian cooks do not put garlic into their traditional tomato sauces, and my version honors the custom.

2 tablespoons butter
2 tablespoons pure olive oil
1 yellow onion, peeled and diced
Kosher salt
4 slices pancetta, cut into ½-inch strips
2 pounds Roma tomatoes, peeled, seeded, and chopped, or 1 28-ounce can Italian-style crushed tomatoes, with their juice
1 teaspoon crushed red pepper flakes
Black pepper in a mill

Heat the butter and olive oil together in a heavy skillet set over medium heat. Add the onion and cook until it is soft and fragrant, about 10 minutes. Season with salt.

Add the pancetta, stir, and cook for 5 to 6 minutes, being careful not to brown the onions. Add the tomatoes and the crushed red pepper flakes and simmer until most of the liquid from the tomatoes has evaporated and the sauce has begun to thicken.

Taste the sauce, correct for salt, and season with several turns of black pepper.

Mexican-Style Summer Tomato Sauce

Makes about 3 cups

Rich, fragrant, and mildly spicy, this sauce is ideal for a broad range of Mexican-style dishes.

3 pounds large red ripe tomatoes
2 or 3 serranos or jalapeños
3 cloves garlic, skin on
1 yellow onion, peeled, cut in
    quarters

4 tablespoons olive oil
½ teaspoon cinnamon
Kosher salt
Black pepper in a mill

Put the tomatoes, chilies, garlic, and onion in a large roasting pan, drizzle a tablespoon of olive oil over them, and toss so that the vegetables are coated with a bit of the oil. Roast the vegetables in a 350°F oven for about 25 minutes, remove from the oven, and let cool until easy to handle. Stem and seed the serranos or jalapeños, remove the skin from the garlic, and place the chilies and garlic in a food processor. Pulse several times to break them up. Pass the roasted onions and tomatoes through a food mill and discard the tomato seeds.

Heat the remaining oil in a heavy skillet, and when it is quite hot carefully pour in the tomato-onion purée all at once, followed by the garlic mixture. Stir the purée well and be sure to scrape up any sauce that has stuck to the bottom of the pan. Add the cinnamon, reduce the heat to low, cover the pan, and cook for 20 minutes, removing the lid and stirring occasionally. The sauce will be very thick and rich. Remove it from the heat and cool slightly. Taste and season with salt and pepper.

This sauce will keep, properly refrigerated, for up to a week and can be frozen.

Winter Tomato Sauce

with Onions, Sage & Pancetta

Makes about 4 cups

This sauce—slightly sweet from the onions and fragrant with the aroma of sage—is ideal for winter pasta dishes.

3 tablespoons butter
4 cups onions, diced (about 5 medium onions)
¼ pound pancetta, diced
2 tablespoons minced fresh sage leaves
28-ounce can chopped or crushed tomatoes
1 tablespoon double-concentrated tomato paste
1 cup homemade chicken stock or water
Kosher salt
Black pepper in a mill
Sage sprigs for garnish

Put the butter into a medium saucepan set over medium heat and, when the butter is melted, add the onions and reduce the heat to low. Cook gently until the onions are very soft and transparent, about 30 minutes. Meanwhile, sauté the pancetta until it loses its raw look and then add it to the onions, along with 1 tablespoon of the sage leaves. Stir and continue to cook over low heat for 10 minutes more.

Stir in tomatoes, tomato paste, and stock or water and simmer for 15 minutes. Taste, correct for salt, season with several turns of black pepper, and stir in the remaining tablespoon of sage. Remove the sauce from the heat and either use immediately or refrigerate. When using the sauce, garnish the dish with the sprigs of sage.

Tomato-Lemon Sauce

Makes 1¾ cups

This is the first tomato sauce I ever made, back when I was a teenager and discovered lamb dolmas swimming in this tangy broth. It was love at first bite and a great sauce for winter, when citrus is in season and tomatoes are not, as you can make it with commercial tomato sauce.

1 cup tomato sauce
¾ cup homemade chicken stock
Juice of 1 lemon
2 teaspoons minced fresh oregano
2 teaspoons freshly ground black pepper
Kosher salt

Heat together the tomato sauce, chicken stock, lemon juice, oregano, and black pepper. Taste the sauce and add salt if necessary. This sauce will keep for up to a week properly refrigerated.

Variations:
- If serving the sauce with lamb, substitute lamb or duck stock for the chicken stock. Reduce the oregano to 1 teaspoon and add ½ teaspoon minced fresh rosemary to the sauce.
- If serving the sauce with beef, use beef stock instead of chicken stock. Vary the herbs according to the herbs in the dish the sauce will accompany.

Dried-Tomato Cream Sauce

Makes about 2 cups

This is a quick, versatile sauce that is excellent with pasta—especially fettuccine or other wide ribbons—and equally good with chicken.

2 cups heavy cream
3 cloves garlic, peeled
2 to 3 sprigs fresh thyme
2 to 3 tablespoons Dried-Tomato Purée (page 53)
¼ cup dry white wine
Kosher salt and freshly ground black pepper

Place the cream, garlic, and thyme in a heavy saucepan over medium heat and reduce the cream by a third. Discard the cloves of garlic and sprigs of thyme. Stir in the dried-tomato purée and the wine and simmer the mixture for about 10 minutes. Season with salt and pepper to taste.

Warm Cherry Tomato Vinaigrette

Makes about ⅔ cup

I use this vinaigrette in a variety of dishes, adding it as a topping for steamed fillets of sole, bitter greens and pasta, and risotto, to name just a few. It is simple to make and provides a great deal of flavor.

1 shallot, minced
2 or 3 garlic cloves, minced
Kosher salt
2 tablespoons white wine vinegar
2 tablespoons fresh lemon juice

⅓ to ½ cup extra-virgin olive oil
1 pint cherry tomatoes, quartered
Black pepper in a mill
2 tablespoons snipped chives or
    chopped Italian parsley

Put the shallot and garlic in a small bowl, add a generous pinch of salt, and add the vinegar and lemon juice. Set aside for 20 minutes.

Pour a little of the olive oil into a sauté pan set over medium heat, add the cherry tomatoes, and sauté for 2 to 3 minutes. Season with a little salt.

Tip in the shallot mixture and the remaining olive oil and heat through.

Remove from the heat, season with several turns of black pepper, and add the chives or parsley.

Taste and correct for salt.

Variations:

- Tomato Wedges: After peeling, cut the tomatoes into quarters. Sauté the tomatoes first, about 30 seconds on each side. Remove them from the pan to a warmed serving bowl. Sauté 1 minced jalapeño pepper along with the shallots. Toss all the ingredients together and use cilantro in place of the mixed herbs.

- With Olives: Add 4 tablespoons Kalamata olives, pitted and coarsely chopped, to the mixture along with the oil, vinegar, lemon juice, and herbs.

Preserving Tomatoes

When you have both an abundance of summer tomatoes and that all-too-rare commodity, time, preserve the harvest by drying, freezing, and canning as much of your crop as possible. The simplest way to do it, which works even when you are pressed for time, is to sear the skins, pack the tomatoes into freezer bags, and pop them into the freezer. You'll use them for sauces and soups all winter. If you have a dehydrator, you can make gorgeous dried tomatoes by using a variety of colors; these tomatoes make perfect snacks. The most traditional method is to can your tomatoes, as has been done for generations.

About Canning

When you are selecting tomatoes for home canning, be sure to keep quality and cleanliness uppermost in your mind. After choosing ripe fruit that is still slightly firm—that is, before the dead-ripe stage—discard any tomatoes with rotten spots, lesions, or splits. Wash the fruit very carefully in fresh water, using several rinses if the tomatoes have gathered soil from the field. Remove the cores of the tomatoes, cut away any green parts, and remove all bruised flesh. Prepare your tomatoes according to the specific recipe, always working on a clean surface and with clean utensils, and then process them as described here. For more detailed information on canning, consult one of the publications listed in the Bibliography (page 311).

Set properly sealed jars in a canning kettle half full of water, and add additional water if necessary to cover the jars two inches above their tops. Turn the heat to high. When the water comes to a rolling boil, reduce the heat to medium and set the timer for forty-five minutes for quarts (thirty-five minutes for pints) of whole tomatoes and tomato sauce, and twenty minutes for quarts (fifteen minutes for pints) of tomato juice. Remove the jars from the canner and gently set them on racks to cool. Check the lids to be sure that they have sealed properly. There will be a slight indentation in the center of lids that have properly sealed. If one is raised, press down; if it stays down, the seal has worked. If it doesn't, reprocess the tomatoes again or refrigerate and use within a few days. Another way to be sure that the seals have worked properly is to tap on them. If the sound they make is sharp and clear, the seal is complete. If the sound is more of a dull thud, the jar is not properly closed and the product will spoil.

Once the jars have fully cooled, store them in a cool, dark cupboard until ready to use.

Canned Tomatoes, Raw Pack
Canned Tomatoes, Hot Pack
Tomato Juice
Oven-Dried Tomatoes

Canned Tomatoes, Raw Pack

Makes about 6 quarts or 12 pints

Use the best-tasting tomatoes available to you, after you have eaten your fill raw, of course. The purpose of canning tomatoes is to preserve the harvest at its peak of flavor to use during the barren months, so there is no need to can early in the season. I believe it is best to can tomatoes in as simple a form as possible, without a lot of other ingredients. That leaves you free to decide how to season each jar of preserved tomatoes as you use it. I do like tucking a basil leaf or two into jars of whole tomatoes, since basil, too, is—or should be—hard to come by in the winter months.

15 pounds of ripe red tomatoes
3 cups, approximately, freshly made Tomato Juice (page 285)
12 fresh basil leaves
½ cup fresh lemon juice

Have a large canning kettle ready, half full of water and on medium-high heat. Peel the tomatoes (see page 41) and remove the cores. Scald 6 quart jars (or 12 pint jars) with boiling water. Pack the tomatoes, either whole or cut in wedges, into the jars, pressing to fill any spaces. Add about ½ cup Tomato Juice if necessary (some varieties of tomatoes will have enough of their own juices) to completely fill in any spaces in the jar and to cover the tomatoes to a half inch below the top. Add 2 basil leaves (1 leaf to pints) and 4 teaspoons of lemon juice to each quart jar, half that amount to pints. Place self-sealing lids and rings on the jars. Process according to instructions on page 281.

Canned Tomatoes, Hot Pack

Makes 6 quarts

This version offers a slight variation of technique.

15 pounds of red ripe tomatoes
12 fresh basil leaves, optional
2 cups, approximately, freshly made Tomato Juice (page 285)
½ cup fresh lemon juice

Have a large canning kettle ready, half full of water and on medium-high heat. Peel the tomatoes (see page 44) and remove the cores. Scald 6 quart jars (or 12 pint jars) with boiling water. Cut the tomatoes in wedges, place them in a large stockpot, and bring them to a boil, stirring regularly so that they do not burn. When they have boiled, pack the hot tomatoes in the scalded jars and top up the jars with the Tomato Juice, if necessary. Add 2 basil leaves (1 leaf to pints), if using, and 4 teaspoons of lemon juice to each quart jar, half that amount to pints. Place self-sealing lids and rings on the jars. Process according to instructions on page 281.

Tomato Juice

Makes about 4 quarts

When you have an abundance of tomatoes from your own garden, you have the luxury of making your own tomato juice.

10 pounds red or golden ripe tomatoes
¼ cup fresh lemon juice
3 teaspoons kosher salt

Have a large canning kettle ready, half full of water and on medium-high heat. Peel the tomatoes (see page 41) and remove the cores. Scald 6 pint jars with boiling water. Cut the tomatoes in half and, to remove the seeds, gently squeeze them over a strainer set over a bowl. Discard the seeds and add the tomatoes and any juices collected in the bowl to a heavy, nonreactive pot set over low heat. Cover the tomatoes and let them simmer slowly for 20 minutes; remove the lid and stir occasionally so that they do not burn.

Let the tomatoes cool slightly and then press them through a food mill. You should end up with about 12 cups of juice. Return the juice to the heat, stir in the lemon juice and salt, and ladle the hot juice into the pint jars, leaving a half inch of room at the top of the jar. Cap with self-sealing lids and rings. Process according to directions on page 281.

Oven-Dried Tomatoes

Makes about 3 dozen dried tomatoes

Before making dried tomatoes, read about it on page 286. This method of drying to-matoes will work best if you have a gas stove with a pilot light. Otherwise, set the controls at the lowest possible temperature.

3 pounds (15 to 18) ripe plum tomatoes

Wash the tomatoes and dry them thoroughly with a tea towel. Cut them in half lengthwise and, using your fingers, very gently scoop out the seeds and gel and discard them. Place the tomatoes, cut side up, on baking sheets and set them in a warm oven. The temperature must never rise over 165°F or the sugar in the tomatoes will burn. Leave the tomatoes in the oven until they are dry and leathery (overnight is ideal). Store them in a cool, dark cupboard and use them within 3 months. Alternately, place the tomatoes in a quart jar and cover them with extra-virgin olive oil.

Beverages

"Everything you see I owe to spaghetti," Sophia Loren has said and as is written in her book *Women & Beauty*.

There were many years that I felt like announcing, whenever I walked off a plane, "Everything you see I owe to a Bloody Mary."

I was once so terrified of flying that it took two Bloody Marys to get me onto a plane. Perhaps ironically, that all changed when the first edition of this book was published and I was sent on a multiple-city book tour. For several years, I traveled so much that I was simply too busy and too tired to focus on my fears. By the time I was touring for *Polenta,* which was published in 1996, I could board a plane without liquid refreshment and even fall asleep before takeoff.

Still, I love a good Bloody Mary, Bloody Maria, or Bloody Miracle now and then, nearly as much as I love a simple glass of tomato juice, which is now my typical in-flight beverage.

You know by now the advice I'm going to offer about making tomato juice at home, don't you? Do it when you have an abundance of backyard or farmers market tomatoes.

Tomato Juice
Tomato Juice Cocktail
Tomato Cucumber Cocktail
Bloody Mary with Variations
Bloody Maria
Bloody Miracle

Tomato Juice

Commercial tomato juice is quite good, full of flavors and textures that are so familiar to us that sometimes a homemade version seems, somehow, wrong. It is another thing entirely, and quite satisfying to make if you have a good supply of garden tomatoes.

5 pounds very ripe tomatoes, peeled, cored, and seeded
1 small red onion, cut in quarters
4 cloves garlic, peeled
2 ribs of celery, with leaves
1 small bay leaf
1 or 2 serranos
4 sprigs of Italian parsley
1 teaspoon whole black peppercorns
Kosher salt
Granulated sugar

Put the tomatoes, onion, garlic, celery, bay leaf, serranos, and Italian parsley in a heavy pot and set over medium heat. When the tomatoes come to a simmer, reduce the heat to low, cover the pot, and cook very gently for 30 minutes. Remove from the heat and let cool for about 15 minutes. Discard the sprigs of parsley, the celery, and the peppers.

Pass the mixture through a food mill or sieve, discard the solids, and chill the juice.

When the juice is thoroughly chilled, taste it and adjust the seasoning with a generous teaspoon of salt and a miserly pinch of sugar. Taste again, and add more salt or sugar as needed for a balanced juice.

Tomato Juice Cocktail

Serves 4

Here's a refreshing drink—mildly spicy and just slightly sweet—for a hot afternoon.

4 cups fresh Tomato Juice (page 285)
1 cup fresh orange juice
Juice of 1 lime
2 tablespoons red wine vinegar
2 cloves garlic, pressed
1 teaspoon celery salt
Several shakes of Worcestershire sauce
Several drops of Tabasco sauce
Kosher salt
Black pepper in a mill
Orange slices or lime slices, for garnish

Combine the juices, vinegar, garlic, celery salt, Worcestershire sauce, and Tabasco sauce in a pitcher, cover, and chill throughly.

To serve, fill tall glasses with ice, pour in the juice, add the garnish, and enjoy. Mix together all the ingredients and taste the juice. Adjust the seasonings for salt, heat, and acid. Chill thoroughly and serve over ice.

Tomato Cucumber Cocktail

Serves 4

Cucumber is one of the most refreshing foods in the world. A few slices in ice water is surprisingly delicious. In this nonalcoholic cocktail, cucumber juice lightens homemade tomato juice for a delicious summer refresher.

4 cups fresh Tomato Juice (page 285)
1 cup fresh cucumber juice (see Note below)
½ teaspoon celery salt
2 teaspoons grated lemon zest
1 tablespoon chives, snipped
Tabasco sauce
Kosher salt and freshly ground black pepper
8 long stalks of chive
12 thin cucumber slices
4 lemon slices

Pour the juices into a pitcher, and add the celery salt, lemon zest, chives, and a shake or two of Tabasco sauce. Season to taste with salt and pepper.

Fill four tall glasses with ice, pour the juice, and garnish with chives, sliced cucumbers, and sliced lemons. Enjoy right away.

NOTE
If you have a juicer, make the cucumber juice according to the manufacturer's instructions. If you do not, peel 2 or 3 large cucumbers and mince them as finely as possible. Set a large strainer over a deep bowl, put the minced cucumbers in the strainer, add a few pinches of salt, and stir now and then.

Bloody Mary
with Variations

Serves 1

One of the most recognizable cocktails in the world, the Bloody Mary is said to have been devised to cure a hangover. Does it? Of course not. Nothing does. But it can make getting through the day a bit easier. I've always thought of the drink as an airport cocktail, as I once needed one or even two to calm my fear of flying. Now, I enjoy a Bloody Mary on a hot summer afternoon or during a winter storm when there is a roaring fire.

Kosher salt
2¼ teaspoons celery salt
Wedge of lemon
2 jiggers (3 ounces) best-quality vodka, chilled
Generous squeeze of fresh lemon juice
Several shakes of Worcestershire sauce
3 or 4 drops Tabasco sauce
1 teaspoon prepared horseradish
8 ounces homemade Tomato Juice (page 285), chilled
¼ teaspoon fine-grain sea salt
⅛ teaspoon black pepper

Use a large (16-ounce) glass to make the Bloody Mary.

Combine the kosher salt with 2 teaspoons of the celery salt in a saucer or shallow bowl. Rub the rim of the glass with the wedge of lemon and dip it into the salt mixture so that it clings to the rim.

Fill the glass with ice. Add the vodka and then the lemon juice, Worcestershire sauce, and Tabasco sauce. Stir in the Tomato Juice with a long spoon. Add the horseradish, sea salt, the remaining celery salt, and pepper.

Stir again and serve.

A Tomato Cookbook

Variations:

- Virgin Mary: Omit the vodka.

- Blondie: For a dazzling visual effect, make the juice using white (they are actually very pale yellow) tomatoes. Omit the Worcestershire sauce and use white pepper instead of black.

Bloody Maria

Serves 1

There are many variations on the classic Bloody Mary, with names like Bloody Geisha, which calls for sake; Bloody Pirate, which uses rum; and Bloody Molly, with Irish whiskey. On and on it goes. My favorite variation replaces traditional vodka with tequila for a delicious lunch cocktail, perfect alongside chips and salsa and spicy egg dishes such as Shakshouka (page 202) and Green Shakshouka (page 205).

Kosher salt in a wide dish
1 teaspoon chipotle powder
½ lime, cut in 2 pieces
2 jiggers (3 ounces) best-quality tequila
2 or 3 drops Habanera hot sauce
1 teaspoon minced fresh cilantro
¼ teaspoon celery salt
Smoked salt, crushed, or fine-grain sea salt
8 ounces Tomato Juice, chilled
Sprig of cilantro, for garnish

Put the kosher salt and chipotle powder into a shallow bowl or small saucepan and use a fork to mix them together well.

Rub the rim of a large glass with a piece of lime and dip it into the salt mixture so that it sticks to the rim.

Fill the glass with ice, add the tequila, followed by the hot sauce, cilantro, celery salt, and salt. Stir with a long spoon, add the Tomato Juice, and stir again. Add a squeeze of the remaining piece of lime, garnish with a sprig of cilantro, and serve immediately.

Bloody Miracle

Serves 4 to 6

This lively cocktail comes to us from The Book of Garlic *(Aris Books, 1974), the classic book on the stinking rose by L. John Harris, writer, publisher, and visual artist, that launched the garlic revolution in the early 1970s. Although you can make a single serving of this delicious cocktail, I recommend preparing a pitcher and enjoying it with friends during a leisurely summer brunch. After trying this version, you may never want another.*

1 lemon, cut in wedges
Kosher salt, for dipping
12 ounces best-quality vodka
6 cloves garlic, pressed
1 tablespoon Tabasco sauce
½ cup fresh lemon juice
2 teaspoons celery salt
1 teaspoon black pepper
1 teaspoon kosher salt
32 ounces (1 quart) Tomato Juice
Sprigs of cilantro

Rub the rims of the glasses with the lemon wedges and then dip them in the kosher salt. Fill a large pitcher half full of ice. Add the vodka, garlic, Tabasco sauce, lemon juice, celery salt, pepper, and kosher salt. Stir the mixture with a long spoon, add the Tomato Juice, and stir again. Garnish each glass with a sprig of cilantro and fill.

Serve immediately.

PART 4
Appendices

Tasting Notes
Commercial Tomato Products
Resources
Bibiliography
Index

Tasting Notes

Tomatoes in Your Garden

Variety _____ Color _____ Source _____

Cost _____ Days to Maturity _____

Appearance_____

Aroma _____

Taste _____

_____

Weight _____ Acid _____ Sugar _____

Skin _____ Texture _____

Problems & Notes

_____

_____

_____

Overall Opinion

_____

_____

Will Grow Again _____

Variety _____ Color _____ Source _____

Cost _____ Days to Maturity _____

Appearance_____

Aroma _____

Taste _____

Weight _____ Acid _____ Sugar _____

Skin _____ Texture _____

Problems & Notes

_____

_____

_____

Overall Opinion

_____

_____

Will Grow Again _____

Variety _____ Color _____ Source _____

Cost _____ Days to Maturity _____

Appearance_____

Aroma _____

Taste _____

Weight _____ Acid _____ Sugar _____

Skin _____ Texture _____

Problems & Notes

_____

_____

_____

Overall Opinion

_____

_____

Will Grow Again _____

Variety _____ Color _____ Source _____

Cost _____ Days to Maturity _____

Appearance_____

Aroma _____

Taste _____

_____

Weight _____ Acid _____ Sugar _____

Skin _____ Texture _____

Problems & Notes

_____

_____

_____

Overall Opinion

_____

_____

Will Grow Again _____

Variety _____ Color _____ Source _____

Cost _____ Days to Maturity _____

Appearance_____

Aroma _____

Taste _____

_____

Weight _____ Acid _____ Sugar _____

Skin _____ Texture _____

Problems & Notes

_____

_____

_____

Overall Opinion

_____

_____

Will Grow Again _____

Variety _____ Color _____ Source _____

Cost _____ Days to Maturity _____

Appearance_____

Aroma _____

Taste _____

_____

Weight _____ Acid _____ Sugar _____

Skin _____ Texture _____

Problems & Notes

_____

_____

_____

Overall Opinion

_____

_____

Will Grow Again _____

Variety _____ Color _____ Source _____

Cost _____ Days to Maturity _____

Appearance_____

Aroma _____

Taste _____

_____

Weight _____ Acid _____ Sugar _____

Skin _____ Texture _____

Problems & Notes

_____

_____

Overall Opinion

_____

_____

Will Grow Again _____

Commercial Tomato Products

**Whole. Ground. Crushed. Diced. Sliced.
Stewed. Sauce. Purée. Paste.**

Product _____ Brand _____

Place of Purchase _____ Cost _____

Appearance_____Aroma_____

Taste _____

Acid _____ Sugar _____

Texture _____

Best Uses

_____

_____

Notes _____

_____

Overall Opinion

_____

_____

Will Purchase Again _____

Product _____ Brand _____

Place of Purchase _____ Cost _____

Appearance_____Aroma_____

Taste _____

Acid _____ Sugar _____

Texture _____

Best Uses

_____

_____

Notes _____

_____

Overall Opinion

_____

_____

Will Purchase Again _____

Product _____ Brand _____

Place of Purchase _____ Cost _____

Appearance_____Aroma_____

Taste _____

Acid _____ Sugar _____

Texture _____

Best Uses

_____

_____

Notes _____

_____

Overall Opinion

_____

_____

Will Purchase Again _____

Product _____ Brand _____

Place of Purchase _____ Cost _____

Appearance_____Aroma_____

Taste _____

Acid _____ Sugar _____

Texture _____

Best Uses

_____

_____

Notes _____

_____

Overall Opinion

_____

_____

Will Purchase Again _____

Product _____ Brand _____

Place of Purchase _____ Cost _____

Appearance_____Aroma_____

Taste _____

Acid _____ Sugar _____

Texture _____

Best Uses

_____

_____

Notes _____

Overall Opinion

_____

_____

Will Purchase Again _____

Product _____ Brand _____

Place of Purchase _____ Cost _____

Appearance_____Aroma_____

Taste _____

Acid _____ Sugar _____

Texture _____

Best Uses

_____

_____

Notes _____

Overall Opinion

_____

_____

Will Purchase Again _____

Product _____ Brand _____

Place of Purchase _____ Cost _____

Appearance_____Aroma_____

Taste _____

Acid _____ Sugar _____

Texture _____

Best Uses

_____

_____

Notes _____

_____

Overall Opinion

_____

_____

Will Purchase Again _____

Resources

C. M. Rick Tomato Genetics
Resource Center
University of California at Davis
Davis, CA
tgrc.ucdavis.edu

This is one of the world's finest repositories of germplasm, with an exhaustive database of wild tomatoes, mutants, cultivars, and more, including digital images, a genebank, extensive information, and lists of available stock.

Kendall Jackson Heirloom Tomato
    Festival
Kendall-Jackson Wine Estate &
    Gardens
5007 Fulton Rd.
Fulton, CA 95439
kj.com

The winery, which grows more than a hundred varieties of heirloom tomatoes on two farms, typically hosts their tomato festival on the last Saturday of September.

Occidental Arts & Ecology Center
15290 Coleman Valley Rd.
Occidental, CA 95482
oaec.org

Doug Gosling has overseen this property's spectacular Mother Garden since the 1980s. Each year, he coordinates three enormous plant sales, one in spring, one in summer, and one in the fall, featuring heirloom species, perennials, medicinal herbs, flowers and more, including scores of tomatoes. This is one of the finest plant sales on the planet and anyone within reasonable driving distance of Sonoma County, California, who has a passion for gardening should check it out.

Seed Savers Exchange
3094 North Winn Rd.
Decorah, Iowa 52101
(563)382-5990
seedsavers.org

A membership organization for gardeners and farmers, with a huge array of seeds and information, available to both members and the general public.

Bibliography

Bailey, Lee. *Tomatoes*. New York: Clarkson Potter, 1992.

Behr, Edward. "A Ripe, Flavorful Tomato." *The Artful Eater*. New York: Atlantic Monthly Press, 1992.

Bittman, Mark. "Which Canned Tomatoes Should You Buy?" *Cook's Illustrated*, March/April 1994.

Colwin, Laurie. "Tomatoes." *More Home Cooking*. New York: Harper-Collins, 1993.

Cool, Jesse Ziff. *Tomatoes: A Country Garden Cookbook*. San Francisco: Collins, 1994.

Cox, Karen. *Just Dried Tomatoes!* Westley, Calif.: Tomato Press, 1989.

della Croce, Julia. "Tomato Sauces for Pasta." *Cook's Illustrated*, March/April 1994.

Editors of Garden Way Publishing. *Tomatoes! 365 Healthy Recipes for Year-Round Enjoyment*. Pownal, Vt.: Storey Communications, 1991.

Estabrook, Barry. *Tomatoland: How Modern Industrial Agriculture Destroyed Our Most Alluring Fruit*. Riverside, New Jersey: Andrews McMeel, 2011.

Foster, Catherine O., ed. *Terrific Tomatoes*. Emmaus, PA.: Rodale Press, 1975.

Gould, Wilbur A. *Tomato Production, Processing, and Technology*. Baltimore: CTI Publications, 1992.

Gray, Patience. *Honey from a Weed*. Berkeley: North Point Press, 1986.

Greene, Janet, Ruth Hertzberg, and Beatrice Vaughan. *Putting Food By*. 4th ed. New York: Penguin Books, 1991.

Grewe, Rudolf. "The Arrival of the Tomato in Spain and Italy: Early Recipes." *Journal of Gastronomy*, Summer 1987.

Hendrickson, Robert. *The Great American Tomato Book*. New York: Stein & Day, 1977.

Hower, George. "*High-Tech Tomato*." Press Democrat (Santa Rosa, Calif.), September 8, 1993.

Jordan, Michele Anna. "Mutant Tomato." *The Paper* (Santa Rosa, Calif.), October 21, 1993.

Kafka, Barbara. "Tomato Times." *The Opinionated Palate*. New York: Morrow, 1992

Kummer, Corby. "Tomato Sauce," *Atlantic*, September 1988.

La Place, Viana. *Unplugged Kitchen*. New York: Morrow, 1996.

Lang, Jennifer Harvey. *Tastings*. New York: Crown, 1986.

Luberman, Mimi. *Terrific Tomatoes*. San Francisco: Chronicle Books, 1994.

Meyer, Scott. "Twilight Zone Tomatoes." *Organic Gardening*, March 1994.

Milioni, Stefano. *Columbus Menu*. New York: Italian Trade Commission, 1992.

Nimtz, Sharon and Ruth Cousineau. *Tomato Imperative!* Boston: Little, Brown, 1994.

Raver, Anne. "Putting Tomatoes to the Taste Test." *New York Times*, September 12, 1993.

Rick, Charles M. "The Tomato." *Scientific American*, August 1978.

Romer, Elizabeth. *The Tuscan Year*. San Francisco: North Point Press, 1989.

_____ *Italian Pizza and Hearth Breads*. New York: Clarkson Potter, 1987.

Seabrook, John. "Tremors in the Hothouse." *New Yorker*, July 19, 1993.

Simeti, Mary Taylor. *On Persephone's Island*. New York: Knopf, 1986.

_____ *Pomp and Sustenance*. New York: Knopf, 1986.

Smith, Andre F. *The Tomato in America Early History, Culture & Cookery*. Columbia: University of South Carolina Press, 1994.

Sokolov, Raymond. *Why We Eat What We Eat*. New York: Simon & Schuster, 1991.

Waldron, Maggie. *Cold Spaghetti at Midnight*. New York: Morrow, 1992.

Waltenspiels, The. *The Sonoma Dried Tomato Cookbook*. Healdsburg, Calif.: Timber Crest Farms, 1992.

Index

Appendices

313

Appendices

Appendices   **317**

Appendices

Appendices

Appendices